THE
SHAAR
PRESS

THE JUDAICA IMPRINT
FOR THOUGHTFUL PEOPLE

WHAT

A SHAAR PRESS PUBLICATION

THE ANGEL TAUGHT YOU

Seven Keys to Life Fulfillment

Rabbi Noah Weinberg
and Yaakov Salomon, C.S.W.

Published by **SHAAR PRESS**
Distributed by MESORAH PUBLICATIONS, LTD.
4401 Second Avenue / Brooklyn, N.Y 11232 / (718) 921-9000

Distributed in Israel by SIFRIATI / A. GITLER
6 Hayarkon Street / Bnei Brak 51127

Distributed in Europe by LEHMANNS
Unit E, Viking Industrial Park, Rolling Mill Road / Jarrow, Tyne and Wear, NE32 3DP/ England

Distributed in Australia and New Zealand by GOLDS WORLD OF JUDAICA
3-13 William Street / Balaclava, Melbourne 3183 / Victoria Australia

Distributed in South Africa by KOLLEL BOOKSHOP
Shop 8A Norwood Hypermarket / Norwood 2196, Johannesburg, South Africa

ISBN: 1-57819-134-3 Hard Cover
ISBN: 1-57819-135-1 Paperback

Printed in the United States of America by Noble Book Press
Custom bound by Sefercraft, Inc. / 4401 Second Avenue / Brooklyn N.Y. 11232

ACKNOWLEGMENTS

"From my teachers I learned a lot, from my colleagues even more, and from my students more than anyone else" *(Talmud Makkos 10a)*.

My father, Rav Yitzchak Mattisyahu Weinberg *zt"l*, asked, "How is it possible for R' Yehudah, a great sage, to state that he learned the *most* Torah from his students?!"

The Talmud *(Sanhedrin 68a)* tells us that the student of a sage can be compared to "a dog who licks water from the ocean." And they were outstanding teachers and students!!

How then could the sage gain the majority of his Torah from those who were able to take only a fraction of what he had?

My father explained that Torah is a gift from the Almighty. Those who undertake to learn it will be blessed with the reward that comes with learning it. But those who undertake to *teach* the Almighty's children will in turn be taught by the Almighty Himself.

It is not the ability of the students that produces the Torah; it is the undertaking to teach them that does.

Therefore, I would like to thank the thousands of students who have studied at Yeshivas Aish HaTorah over the last thirty years. It is their burning desire (albeit sometimes unconscious) to reconnect with their heritage that compelled me to undertake articulating the beauty, relevance, and power of Judaism to a generation of estranged, skeptical, and sometimes even antagonistic students.

Furthermore, I would like to thank all those who have taught these concepts in this format, or developed their own classes, books, and seminars, from these core ideas, in an effort to connect Jews throughout the world with *Toras Chaim*.

Of course, Aish HaTorah would not even exist without the support of the generous contributors — too numerous to mention. I thank them for making the vision of Aish HaTorah a reality.

I would also like to thank Rabbi Yitzchok Coopersmith who drafted the lectures from which much of this material was collected.

My appreciation goes to my co-author, R' Yaakov Salomon, whose warm, wise, and beautiful writing has enhanced the presentation immeasurably.

Finally, I would like to express my *hakaras hatov* to my dear wife Dinah, who has been behind me every step along the way.

Noah Weinberg

Kislev 5764

It's ironic.

The first thing many book readers actually glance at is the section on acknowledgments — it appears in the front. But the acknowledgments are usually written last. After the author has completed his manuscript, he has a fuller appreciation of all the work he has put in and, in turn, for all the people who have really contributed in some way.

And so it is. The people who contributed to this project, I realize now, are not only those who directly reviewed, revised, and criticized my writing, but also those who have helped shape my interests, philosophies, and skills through the years. They have a share in any impact this book makes.

There are very very few visionaries in this world. Dreamers — there are plenty. But Rabbi Noah Weinberg is a true visionary. Meeting R' Noah is a delight; studying his teachings is a privilege; understanding the depth of his genius is a thrill. But being asked to elucidate and expand upon his understanding of life is an honor I will always cherish. My association with this Torah giant, and his hand-picked generals and lieutenants, has changed nearly every aspect of my life. I hope to someday be a visionary too. My thanks is boundless.

One of the highest ranking generals is Rabbi Yitzchok Coopersmith. Mentor, collaborator, and *chavrusa*, R Yitzchok's clarity and creativity are surpassed only by his humility and disdain for the limelight. Many of the concepts you will read about were either created or enhanced by him. I'm always learning from you, Yitzchok. I hope.

My Rav, Rabbi Hillel David *shlita*, has quietly steered the Salomon ship for over thirty years. Through direct sagacious counsel and constant role modeling, he, along with Rav Dovid Cohen *shlita*, has deftly kept me on course, frequently despite my own best intentions. I am indebted to them both.

I first met Rabbi Nosson Scherman when I was an over-ambitious adolescent in Camp Torah Vodaath — training grounds for scores of future personalities in Jewish communal life. If I was impressed by him then (and I was), I am awed by him now. His editing of this manuscript and the many cogent suggestions he offered, are just the most recent in a long list of contributions he has made to me. Role model, mentor, advisor, editor, and *chavrusa* — he has played a central role in my life. Thank you. Of course, a special thanks to you, Reb Nosson and to Rabbi Meir Zlotowitz and the entire staff for adding a new rung to our ladder of mutual association. Your confidence in this project is greatly appreciated.

Eighteen years ago, when I sought a suitable learning environment, Hashem steered me into the holy confines of Yeshivah Torah Vodaath. The *roshei yeshivah* and *rebbeim* there have been more than generous in sharing their extraordinary knowledge and life experiences with me.

In particular, my fellow *kollel* members — Rabbis Heshy Wolf, Moshe Lamm, Moshe Yehuda Szwerin, Yoni Levinson, and Sholom and Zev Smith — have kindly treated me like a peer instead of a *talmid*. But I know the truth. I thank them all.

I have also been blessed with outstanding and patient *chavrusos*: Chaim Shmeel Friedman, Chaim Goldbaum, Dr. Chaim Weiss, and Chaim Finn (apparently only "Chaims" need apply). I'd be lost without each of you.

Dr. Meir Wikler is another *chavrusa*, but has been, for more than thirty years, much more than that. Thank you for your loyalty, availability, counsel, laughs, and love.

My involvements with Aish HaTorah and the DISCOVERY program have enriched my life, broadened my perspectives, and altered my priorities. I know of no single group of individuals that is more dedicated, talented, and invested in the future of the Jewish people than my exceptional colleagues on the DISCOVERY circuit: Max Anteby, Shlomie Berger, Eliyahu Bergstein, Heshey Gans, Yossi Glatstein, Andy Goldfinger, Yitz Greenman, Daniel Mechanic, Yerachmiel Milstein, Rick Probstein, Hertzy Tepfer, and Chaim Weiss. All of you share in this book.

How often do we find something we love to do, yet never seem to make the time or find the opportunity to actually do it? Rabbi Nechemia Coopersmith became the solution to my writing resistance by providing the perfect forum for my musings and by constantly coaxing me to return to the keyboard. His innovative and stimulating aish.com website, which he runs along with Rabbi Shraga Simmons, is visited 1.2 million times per month. Keep pushing me.

Rabbi Paysach Krohn may be the busiest Jew I know. Somehow he fits me into his schedule — practically every day. No idea or project of mine, serious or trivial, goes unfiltered by his sensitive soul and passionate perception. Thanks for everything.

This book is one of the few major projects that I did without Rabbi Yonah Weinrib. But everything I do has his unique mark on it, in some way. His creativity, erudition, and unremitting energy and faith have inspired everyone. I treasure our friendship.

Dr. David Lieberman, valued friend, inspiration, and author of note, graciously advised and encouraged me since this project started over two years ago. Thanks.

It seems so farcical to attempt to find the adequate expressions to properly thank Hashem for His unvarying guidance throughout this undertaking. No greater pleasure exists than the incomparable feeling that Hashem is in your constant awareness — directing and supervising your every move. My hope is that this awareness will grow and flourish and allow me to see His hand everywhere.

Perhaps the greatest example of perceiving His hand is the unparalleled feeling I get watching my family grow and develop. My mother and my in-laws שיחיו are superlative captains of the ship; my brother Izzy, and his family, live with incredible passion and pride; my children and grandchildren are my most precious gifts; and my wife Temmy never ever ever stops giving. Collectively, your love and unwavering support are what keep me afloat.

And thanks to all my readers. I'd love to hear from you.

Yaakov Salomon
ysalomon@aish.com

Kislev 5764

CONTENTS

AUTHORS' INTRODUCTION

Something very strange is going on in this world.

- The more knowledge we accumulate, the more confused we get.
- The more conveniences we invent, the less time we seem to have.
- The more we know about love, the less satisfying our relationships become.
- The more pleasures we create, the more pain we need to confront.

The questions appear to engulf us. The answers seem so elusive. We run. Sometimes physically, sometimes mentally. We hide. Or at least we try to. But more often than not, the questions come with us. Gnawing at us, reminding us that we are not really at peace. When contradictions abound, we are perplexed and in need of direction, clarity, and understanding.

The voices within us never really go away. The "mute" button may be on and the "white noise" might be deafening, but the doubts still lurk in the distance and the uncertainties never really fade away.

- *When will I be truly happy with my life?*
- *Can I really trust my beliefs?*
- *How do I know if my decisions are the right ones?*
- *What is the definition of "love"?*
- *How do I get my prayers answered?*
- *Why doesn't money bring me more pleasure?*
- *Is life pre-ordained or do I determine what happens to me?*
- *Are there absolute truths in this world or only people's "perceptions"?*

Believe it or not, according to Jewish thought and tradition, you don't have to search far for the answers. *You already have them!* The answers to these and all the other questions you may ask are closer than you think. Permit me to explain.

According to the Talmud, before we were born, when we were safely ensconced in the comfort of the womb, we all had access to the ultimate search engine. God dispatches a personal angel to each and every soul in utero, and this angel sits beside each and every one of us, and actually teaches us *all* the wisdom we will ever need to know on this planet. Everything.

And then…just before we are born…the angel gives us a little "tap" between the nose and the upper lip and everything he taught is immediately forgotten. That is how all human beings receive that small indentation in the skin beneath the nose, anatomically known as the "philtrum."

▶ Why bother?

"**S**trange story," you say. And who could blame you? First of all, how do we know that angels exist? And second, why would God send an angel to teach us everything we need to know, only to instruct him to then make us forget everything he just taught us? What would be the point?

Proving the existence of angels is not an easy chore, nor is it the purpose of this book. However, if we believe in God (and four out of five people say they do believe in some kind of deity), trusting that He would have some kind of ministering work-corps is certainly not very far removed.

More perplexing is question number two. Why bother to teach us everything, only to erase our memory chip immediately afterwards?

The answer, like most answers after we know them, is really rather simple. The best way to acquire real knowledge and to retain it is through self-exploration. The facts and the understanding with which we become most proficient are those that we ourselves have studied, researched, or experienced personally. Wisdom that is spoon-fed to us or acquired secondhand is not nearly as clear or as functional. Hence, allowing us to keep the knowledge we learned in the womb would surely not be in our best interests. If so, why bother teaching it to us in the first place? Because learning something once makes it so much easier for us to learn it for the second time.

Life is so very complex. Knowing all there is to know in order to navigate through this world safely, productively, and pleasurably is a daunting task. God says, "Let Me help you out a little. Learn about your destination before you embark on the journey. That way, when you get there, you'll have a head start." Everything will seem just a little bit familiar to you. Instead of starting from scratch, and scratching from the start, you will be reviewing, so to speak, everything you already knew.

What a novel concept! Perhaps this is what King Solomon was alluding to when he proclaimed in Ecclesiastes, "There is nothing new under the sun." Once we are born and live "under the sun," we have already been exposed to everything we need to know. So there really is nothing we can learn that is new to us.

▶ Why is this so important?

Before we can answer life's questions about happiness, beliefs, love, prayer, absolute truth, etc., we must first clear a path — a path that fosters openness and authenticity, a path that allows us to examine truth in a light that is truly objective and dispassionate. And for that to happen, we need to understand the building blocks of the human experience.

Five billion people inhabit this earth. No two are the same. Diversity is present in every facet of our existence. And yet, there are certain tools to understanding mankind that are truly universal. There are mechanisms at play that cut across all lines of difference — racial, cultural, religious, biological, characterological — all components of the human species. Let us examine these fundamental truths, remembering all along that we are not seeing them for the first time, but rather reconnecting to a knowledge base that we encountered long before our conscious awakening.

▶ The ABC's

AThe first primary concept of these foundations of life, or ABC's of human understanding, is the appreciation of where our personal values and beliefs about life really come from. We would all like to think that each one of us has formed his or her own belief system based on independent and unbiased perceptions and experiences. After all, who would allow a prejudiced view or ideal to influence the formation of the core of one's character or values?

And yet, the truth parks itself very far from that curb. The sad reality is that we are all creatures of the society in which we live. And the influence that our surroundings have on our ideas about life and the way we live every day is both immeasurable and unavoidable.

- *How do we decide what is right and what is wrong?*
- *What is considered "acceptable behavior"?*
- *How do we distinguish between a "good thing to do" and a genuine priority?*

- *What really dictates our dress code, lifestyle, and occupational choices?*

The list goes on and on. Fact is, the collective consciousness of any culture is communicated to its constituents through the books and periodicals they read, the visual media that is broadcast, the educational system that is employed, and the socio-economic and political messages that are promulgated. Some of the messages are direct; others are discreet. All are powerful. Try, as we do, to shield ourselves from the raging forces of partiality, we fail. How we shape our thinking is, surprisingly, often not more than a mere accident of birth.

There are exceptions. But chances are, no matter what you believe right now, if you were born into a religious family in Haiti, you would be sticking pins in voodoo dolls. If Teheran was your city of birth, you might very well be a devout follower of an Ayatollah of some kind. Sure, radicals emerge in every society, but for the most part, we do follow some party line.

This sorry state of affairs should irk every one of us! How do we pretend to objectively determine reality? How is it possible for any self-respecting individual to discern who he really is and what he should believe in?

The solution

The solution to this problem is staring you right in the face...literally! The answer is right under your nose. Yes. The philtrum. It wasn't enough for your angel to teach you all about life. Nor was his job completed when he made sure you then forgot everything he taught you. There was one final step remaining. He had to leave his "calling card" with you so that the only thing you would remember was that he was there.

The philtrum was the angel's very personal way of leaving a message behind. "When you seek the truth and feel like the search may be a lost cause, just run your finger over your lips, close your mouth and feel the 'impression' that was made on you. Do not despair. You'll recognize reality when you see it. After all, you already found and understood it before."

We enter this world fully equipped with wisdom. The soul knows everything there is to know about life. What holds us back from being fully objective and independent is not the difficulty in learning what reality is, but rather the effort we need to exert to access what we already know. All three dimensions are really on the screen; we just forget to put on the 3-D glasses!

In other words, there is no clear-cut formula for figuring out which ideas and values are truly bona fide and which are ultimately invalid. But that by no means implies that we are discouraged from conducting the examination. Quite the contrary! Making the effort to scrutinize, and having the wherewithal to demand clarity, is precisely how the truth will emerge. Living in a semi-comatose existence of blind acceptance of the beliefs of our neighbors, columnists, and yes, even our clergy, is just grazing with the rest of the herd.

This is the true challenge for every one of us. If we commit ourselves to the task of sorting through the muck and the marketing, and become ardent truth-seekers, we can actualize our full potential as human beings on this planet. It is only through this critical analysis that we can say we have lived life to its fullest.

The good news is that we already have a head start — the philtrum.

BFolks are fond of saying,"Life is complicated." But I've heard it said that life is really quite simple; it's the people who are complicated. And it's true. The mystery of what makes a man or a woman tick will surely be considered until the end of time.

But one fundamental truth about the human condition can be stated with certainty; and this can be identified as the "B" in our schemata of the ABC's of human understanding. There is only one major factor, endemic to all people throughout all of time, which dictates our every move and motivates us in every decision we make. And that is pleasure.

Every single time we are faced with a choice of what to do, be it something crucial and monumental or something trivial and inconsequential, we always ask ourselves, "Will this bring me pleasure or not?" Sometimes the question is asked consciously, sometimes not. Sometimes the choice is rather obvious; other times it is exceedingly subtle. But always, what we end up doing is determined by what action will result in the ultimate greater pleasure. Keep in mind that the particular pleasure may not be immediate. It may even appear to be more painful than pleasurable (at the moment). But the evaluation will still boil down to an assessment of the potential for pleasure.

Why pleasure?

Ask any parent: "What do you really want for your children?"

No matter which culture you are in, you are bound to hear the very same answers from all parents. They want them to be healthy, strong, full of joy and vitality, accomplished, attractive, confident, popular, maybe even rich, etc. But why do they want all these things for their children? One answer: because these are all ingredients for happiness. Every parent wants his or her child to be happy, full of pleasure — the maximum pleasure. When their children are happy, the parents are energized. If the children are sad and miserable, the parents can go out of their wits.

In Judaism, and later in all religions, God is referred to as "Our Father in Heaven." We are referred to as His children. Just as a parent only wants his children to be happy, so does God only want His children to be happy. It is clear that this is the reason we were created — to get the most out of life.

Of course, pleasure is a very relative term. People experience pleasure in many, many different forms. And, as they say, "to each his own." However, if I told you that my neighbor's son enjoys playing with Lego very much, you would have no problem with that. If I then told you that he plays with Lego 16 hours a day that might be problematic to you. And if I later informed you that my neighbor's son was 32 years old, you would be unlikely to respond, "Oh, whatever makes him happy, I guess." Especially if you were his father!

Why not? Probably because everyone realizes that there exists on this world an incredibly wide range of pleasurable experiences. We want our children to not only be happy, but also to enjoy what we call "a full life." And the assumption is that "a full life" is a lot more pleasurable than one limited only to Lego, backgammon, or video games. There's love, meaning, creativity, religion, the joy of giving, and so on. But more on that later.

Check it out...

Meanwhile, let us apply the "A" principle to the "B" principle. We are stating that the driving force behind our decision-making apparatus is the quest for pleasure, be it immediate or eventual. But how do we know this is true? Let us not blindly accept this premise on face value. Without proper investigation, we could be accepting a false reality. What method would we use in order to determine the intended utility of any item? Primarily, we would examine its construction. We see a knife. We take note (carefully now) of the sharpness of the blade. We conclude, correctly, that it is made for cutting purposes.

Now, pretend that you have never before seen a ballpoint pen. Someone shows you the pen and tells you it is a toothpick. You would say, "Ridiculous! Toothpicks do not have ink in them (among a host of other obvious differences)." So he changes his mind and tells you the pen is really a very small car. "Impossible," you say, "Where's the sunroof and CD player?"

With very little effort you could discern that the pen is, in fact, a pen. You examine the structure of the item and know that it is designed to write with, because that is what it does best. That's what the parts seem to indicate.

Now let's take a look at how human beings were constructed.

Our day is filled with decisions, thousands of them, but most we make subconsciously: what time to wake up, what to wear, the breakfast menu, whether to answer the phone, how to travel, work-related judgments, social commitments, etc. And many factors are involved in our evaluations of what we should do.

Primarily, however, in every case we are really deciding what will bring us the most pleasure.

Let's take a closer look. It's 7 a.m. The alarm clock rings. You shut it. Now...do you get out of bed or not? Somewhere, in the deep, sleepy recesses of your mind you are asking yourself, "What is my pleasure?" If your decision is to sleep some more, you hug the pillow. But if you decide that going to work will really bring you more pleasure (eventually), you'll get up right away. We may call it "obligation" or "responsibility," but, in fact, it is our assessment that being responsible will result in more overall pleasure that motivates us to get up and go.

Of course, often times the appearance of pain or effort serves to obfuscate our vision, and cloak the pleasure in shrouds of exertion. That is when we fall victim to the trap of making the "wrong decision," and avoid effort at any cost. But clearly, pleasure is the ultimate yardstick. This applies whether we are deciding which pajamas to buy, whom to marry, or what career to choose. If it promises pleasure and enjoyment, we'll pursue it. That's the way human beings are wired.

We are all pleasure seekers. Even when we do something altruistic, we do it because it gives us pleasure. Even when we restrain and restrict ourselves from a certain pleasure, it too is because of our judgment that this particular restriction is "good" for us. And "being good" is a great pleasure.

Curiously, this is exactly the way God wants us to be. We know this to be true because that is exactly how He programmed each and every one of us. Sometimes we mistakenly forget that this world, which He created, affords us endless opportunities for pleasurable experiences. We focus on the pain, the effort, the hardships, and the suffering that frequently appear inexplicable. These inevitable distractions deflect our attention from the fact that pleasure drives every move we make. That is not a human weakness or accident; it is a Heavenly design for mankind.

Therefore, if you find yourself unhappy, or not as happy as you should be, it behooves you to ask, "Why not? What is blocking my path to real and lasting happiness?" More than likely, the problem lies in your not having learned all the pleasures that are available to you in this world. You just don't know where or how to get the kinds of pleasure that will be ultimately satisfying — the kinds of pleasure for which all of us are truly searching.

Later on we will discuss the different classes of obtainable pleasure, how to recognize them, access them, and avoid the pitfalls that impede our means to reach them. Meanwhile, let us understand that just as our parents want us to enjoy our lives, so too does God want His children to get the maximum pleasure out of life. We just have to find out how to do it. That is the goal. God made this world to give us pleasure. That is the "B" of our model.

C Now...here is something puzzling. All the systems seem to be in place. God only wants to give us pleasure. We are programmed to receive pleasure. And yet, so many of us are bored, dissatisfied, or just plain miserable! How are we to understand this? What is getting in the way?

Judaism teaches us that we are geniuses at making mistakes. We get confused. We err. We miss the mark. Our mistakes in judgment cause us to severely limit the amount of pleasure we can derive. The missteps of man do not come about because we are sinners; rather, it is because we are mistake prone. And there is a big difference. That is the "C" of human understanding.

Deep down, everyone truly wants to be good. Everyone wants pleasure. But we err in our evaluation of how to get it. We forget how much effort it sometimes takes to see the benefits and rewards of our toil. Instead, we often choose short-cuts, which sometimes can work, but more frequently leave us depressed and bewildered. "What happened to my marriage?" we ask. "Why did this great relationship end? Where did my kids go wrong? Why don't I have meaning in my life? How did I end up in this dead-end job anyway? Why am I so unlucky?"

We want a thriving family life, but forget the overwhelming need for commitment and investment of time and effort. We claim to long for meaning, but then fall prey to social pressures that attach importance only to the facade of success. We want to live compatibly with everyone, but never lay the groundwork for the methodology of avoiding arguments.

For example...

Picture the following all-too-common scenario: Marty, 16, has just walked into the house at 2:45 a.m., two hours past his curfew. It is his third violation this month. Dad, awakened by the slamming car door, comes storming down the stairs to confront him. He is clearly at the end of his rope. In seconds, the situation erupts.

"You're driving me crazy, Marty. What in heaven's name is wrong with you? Are you trying to give me a heart attack?"

What is the response Dad is hoping to get from his sincere plea for sanity? What does he want to hear from Marty?

"Gee Dad, I never thought about it that way. You make an excellent point. That's just the message I needed to hear now. On the basis of your powerful and persuasive argument, I've just decided to turn over a new leaf and do something really meaningful with my life."

What are the chances of that happening? Right. Zero. And yet Dad must believe, on some level, that his tirade is going to work? What a mistake! A far more likely response from Marty might be:

"Listen, Dad, I'm in no mood to listen to you. Fact is that you made a mess out of your own life. You never had time for me and you never really loved me, so just stay out of my life."

Now, I suppose Marty is expecting a reply to that, resembling...

"Son, I am really impressed with you. You are very perceptive. I especially admire how you don't let anyone push you around — even me! I want you to know that I am behind you 100 percent!"

Not in a million years! And yet, we all make mistakes like this all the time.

What is going on here? Dad just wants Marty to show a little respect. He really wants to be close to his son, but hasn't a clue how to achieve that. Marty's needs are not very different. He would treasure a closer relationship with his father, but also wants to be allowed to express his independence. They need each other. They want each other. But they are badly mistaken in how to go about creating a relationship that never really got off the ground.

Our lives are full of mistakes. But don't confuse mistakes with accidents. Mistakes can be avoided. We don't have to put others down to raise our own self-esteem. We can commit ourselves to diet and exercise. We can learn that getting even brings us only to a warped sense of temporary satisfaction. We are able to understand what our life's priorities should be.

But steering clear of these crucial mistakes in life requires perception, commitment, and mostly, hard work. With proper focus we can ensure that the pleasure we ultimately desire can actually be attained.

And one more thing...

Above all, if we sincerely want to stay away from a lifelong pattern of repetitive and catastrophic blunders, we must avoid the number one mistake in life. And that is the mistake of ignorance.

Ignorance is really the foundation of all mistakes. People ruin their lives out of ignorance. They cheat. They under-achieve. They berate. They complain. They pretend. They even murder — physically, emotionally, and spiritually. Why? Because they don't understand. They don't know what true pleasure is. They never learned how to enjoy life to the fullest — in fulfilling and long-lasting ways. And so, out of confusion and ignorance, they react, without giving serious thought to the implications of their decisions.

Everyone knows that getting an education is important. But is education limited to calculus, literature, microbiology, and quantum physics? Shouldn't we know more than how the process of osmosis works, the trajectory of planetary orbits, and when and why Australia was torn off the Indian continent?

It's nice to know all these things, but when all is said and done, we still need to know who we are, why we were created, and what we are living for. Somewhere along the way, we seem to have lost the forest for the trees. The bottom line is...if we don't know ourselves, we know nothing. And the greatest pleasures in the world will elude us.

We need to re-educate. In this book, we will attempt to do that. The philtrum holds the answers to the questions we really should be asking: about life, meaning, clarity, love, purpose, prayer, free will, etc.

Let us reconnect and rediscover the answers that will bring us clear, true, and lasting happiness.

Let's begin.

THE FIVE LEVELS OF PLEASURE

1

Several times a year, I become a millionaire. And, chances are, so do you. Well...not exactly. But you and I receive frequent letters congratulating us on becoming a "Grand Prize Sweepstakes Winner!" of some kind. Occasionally we win $10 million; other times it's a luxury cruise around the world. Sometimes we are offered a "free" sports car or perhaps a yacht or a chalet in the mountains.

For a second, or a fraction thereof, our hearts flutter. "Could this one be for real?" we pretend. "Hey! Somebody out there probably wins these things," we declare playfully. Then we look for the fine print. Inevitably, it is there. Sometimes it is hiding in convoluted prattle or incoherent legalese, and sometimes it barely approaches microscopic size, but it is there. The prize is only available to "members" of a club to which you don't belong, you're being congratulated on becoming a "finalist" (along with 19 million others), the prize is not 10 million — it is "UP TO 10 million," etc.

We learn the lesson rather quickly. Nothing is for nothing. If somebody is handing out $100 bills on the street…look out!

Let's expand this notion to life itself. Everyone who has been born has been endowed with incredible gifts — sight, hearing, understanding, imagination, relationships, and so on. The list, if we would ever find the time and courage to make it, is truly endless. All of us have really won the Grand Prize! In the "sweepstakes" of life, we are all winners. Instinctively then, we must now ask the obvious questions:

- *What's the catch?*

- *Where's the fine print?*

- *What "club" must I join?*

- *How much will this "victory" cost me?*

- *What does God want or expect in return for all He has given me?*

These are all reasonable questions. It makes sense to want to know what God really wants from us. The answer to that most poignant question can serve as a true guide for how we should live our lives.

The answer, however, is rather shocking. It can best be expressed in one seven-letter word:

Nothing.

That's right. Nothing. There is no fine print or legal gobbledygook. No club to join or dues to pay. God wants nothing from us. He hands us the greatest gift possible — life, and wants nothing in return.

Simple logic tells us how true and obvious this is. By definition, God is perfect. The Creator of the world is the embodiment of precision and flawlessness. A perfect being cannot "want" anything. He has no needs, no wants. He *IS* EVERYTHING! To presume that God could "want" is to declare that he is not God at all.

With infinite wisdom, he created DNA, brain synapses, and billions of fingerprints, each one unique. He placed the earth exactly 93 million miles away from the sun, the perfect distance. He made watermelon fiery red and snowflakes linen white. What could He possibly want from us?

God cannot want or need anything. It is we mortals who need things. We mistakenly think that He needs us to fulfill His will or listen to His commandments in order to satisfy His needs.

It is clear that there is nothing that we could give to an all-powerful, all-knowing God; which brings us to an even more compelling question: If He wants nothing from us, why did He bother to create this world? If we are not here to give to Him, what then is our purpose on this planet?

Logic again leads us to the only possible conclusion. If we are not here to give, we must be here only to receive, to accept God's incredible array of gifts and make certain that we avail ourselves of their benefit to the absolute maximum degree. That is our purpose — to bask in all the opportunities for enjoyment and access the ultimate pleasure possible.

Incredible! All our lives we are taught the lessons of the beauty of giving, and all God wants is for us to be "takers"? Can this be true?

It sure can. In fact, when we become real connoisseurs of pleasure, we are fulfilling our life goals to the greatest degree. Of course, a real connoisseur is never satisfied with inferior grades of the product in which he is involved. He insists on constantly upgrading his menu until he reaches the zenith of his experiences. A wine expert would never be content with drinking Malaga, no matter how good it tasted at the moment. He understands that grapes far more complex and robust await his exploration and scrutiny. Similarly, a pleasure specialist knows that solitaire, fast cars, and sushi are all marvelous creations, but they hardly represent the apex of pleasurable experiences in this world.

It is as if God is saying, "The repertoire of delight and satisfaction that I have prepared for you is infinitely elaborate. And you have been programmed to seek out the experiences that bring you joy. Your task is to become an authority on every single aspect of every single pleasure. Don't get stuck playing with Lego every day. Your constructions may be extremely creative, but your energy level is bound to collapse."

▸ Why parents?

Realizing that part and parcel of being the entity of perfection is the necessity to share all the goodness, God set out to fashion a world with beings that could receive His gifts and appreciate their inherent qualities. But how should these beings be created? Shall they grow on trees? Be hatched from eggs? Become amoeba-like, self-reproducing organisms? A perfect method had to be devised in order for these creatures to best understand their role in this giant schemata we call "life."

And so, the parental process was born. With wisdom well beyond our comprehension, God "understood" that we could best ascertain what exactly He wanted for us, by our having a relationship paradigm to which we could relate and from which we could learn. God is also a parent, but without all the baggage. When we experience the love, devotion, and commitment in a healthy parent-child connection, we may begin to fathom what it is that God, as our "Father in heaven," wants for us too.

As explained earlier (see Introduction), parents usually have a long list of dreams for their growing children. But ultimately, what every parent wants most for his children is for them to be happy. When a parent sees his children happy, he is filled with contentment. But if a parent sees his children miserable, he shares and often exceeds their misery with overwhelming despair and sadness of his own. Such is the nature of the world as we know it.

Perhaps that is why every child and every toddler in this universe reacts in exactly the same way when he wants something from his parents. When all the reasoning, arguing, and pleading have failed, he resorts to crying. No matter what culture that child is from, he seems to know instinctively that withholding pleasure from his parents is a methodology worth pursuing. Why does he cry? It's really very simple — it's extremely effective!

"If I can just demonstrate to them that I am not happy," he reasons, "they'll cave in." And, more often than not, it works.

God is no different. He is perfect; He wants nothing at all from us. All He created us for is to benefit from His vast range of pleasures. When we do that, the purpose of creation has been achieved.

▸ Five Different Levels

All of life's pleasures can be classified within five distinct levels or categories. If our goal is to experience the maximum benefit from all of life's treasures (and it is), then we must understand the hierarchy of these categories. We need to know which of the pleasures have more potential to bring us gratification so that we can concentrate our attention on those engines that contain the most "horsepower." No one in his right mind would prefer to spend 8 hours on an airplane sitting in a middle seat near the rear lavatory, if he were offered a seat in First Class for the same price. The journey through life follows the same reasoning. Since no two experiences carry with them the identical power for satisfaction, evaluating pleasure potential becomes one of life's most essential prerequisites.

The measure of pleasure

Understanding how to measure pleasure is not easy. Some activities seem like "fun." Others give us a "high." There are those that appear to give us a "physiological lift." How can we know which pleasures are truly more valuable than others?

One way is to define pleasure in units of energy. When you have real pleasure you feel energized — ready to tackle anything and confident that no task is beyond your reach. Your frustration tolerance level is elevated and your perseverance knows no bounds. And the feeling lasts. We've all had experiences that generated an unusual amount of vitality and confidence. That is real pleasure.

We can also measure pleasures by prioritizing them. In our scheme of ordering the pleasures into five different classes, we can see that there is really no exchange rate from one class to another. In other words, if we call fifth level the lowest class of pleasure, and work up the ladder toward first level, we will see that no reasonable person would exchange even a tiny amount of fourth-level pleasure in order to obtain large amounts of fifth- level pleasure. Each higher level is unique and on a totally different plain than the level preceding it. By observing our actions we can actually recognize the relative worth we place on our experiences. More on that later.

▶ Criteria for enjoyment

Before detailing the five different classes of pleasure, we need to identify three prerequisites for enjoying pleasure at any level.

1. Become a connoisseur

In a wine-tasting course, they teach you that a glass of wine is far more than just another liquid that wets your mouth. There are a whole variety of pleasures that are available in every glass of wine. There is the bouquet, the color, the texture, and many areas of your mouth with which to taste the wine, each part giving you a totally different savory experience. Similarly, life offers a lot of different opportunities for pleasure. A beautiful day could give you hours of pleasure if you sensitize yourself to all of its exquisite details. Without learning how to do that, however, its beauty may give you a lift only for a matter of minutes and then the feeling is gone.

Within each level of pleasure, you have to learn how to appreciate and enjoy the pleasure available to you; otherwise, you cannot access the pleasure. Just like someone cannot fully appreciate the pleasures of a glass of wine without a wine-tasting course, or the painting of a great master without an art-appreciation class, a human being cannot fully enjoy the entire spectrum of pleasures that are available in life unless he knows what those pleasures really are.

Don't accept any pleasure on face value alone. Attempt to define what each pleasure brings to the table. Identify why this particular experience is generating energy for you. And then explore the depths of enjoyment that may not be immediately perceptible.

2. Focus on the pleasure, not the effort

It is easy to forget that every pleasure you want in life has a price tag attached to it. That price tag is effort. The greater the pleasure, the greater the effort needed to acquire it. Superficial pleasures require far less effort in order to attain them. To truly appreciate each level of pleasure, you have to learn to focus on the pleasure and not on the price you are paying to get it. If you focus on the pleasure, you won't even notice the effort. But if you focus on the effort, you may miss the pleasure completely.

Take a group of teenagers who love to play basketball. On a warm Sunday afternoon, they might play ball for 2 or 3 hours without interruption. Perhaps even more. But what would happen if you asked them to conduct the following experiment?

> *Play basketball as you would normally, but with*
> *one slight alteration; we are going to take away the*
> *ball. Continue to run, jump, shoot, rebound, and*
> *play defense, as you would if you were really play-*
> *ing with a ball. I'll tell you when to stop.*

For how long do you think they could play? Three minutes? Five minutes? Before too long, all they would notice is the effort involved in the exercise.

> *Hey! This is tiring!*
> *Boy, it's hot out here!*

But just give them back the ball, and they will continue to play for 2 hours or more. Heat? Fatigue? No longer a factor.

In life, you have to keep your eye on the ball. You have to learn to focus your attention on the pleasure. When you do, the effort is hardly noticeable. If you do not focus on the pleasure, however, it's like taking away the ball from the basketball game. Suddenly every move is laden with sweat and exertion.

In every category of pleasure you have a choice: Focus on the pleasure or focus on the effort. Focus on the effort, and you won't even want to get out of bed. Focus on the pleasure, and no amount of hard work will ever deter you.

3. Counterfeit pleasures

The third prerequisite is to beware of counterfeit pleasures. Just as there is counterfeit money in this world — it looks great and feels real — there is also counterfeit pleasure. People make mistakes all the time thinking they're going to have pleasure, but somehow they often wind up with something far less.

Within each level of pleasure there is a counterfeit experience that says, "Come! Invest your time and energy trying to attain me." In the end, though, you are duped by an illusion masquerading as the true pleasure.

The pursuit of pleasure should be treated as serious business, and you have to be businesslike in your effort to achieve it. If someone came into your office and said, "I have a great idea to help you make $10 million. Just invest a few hundred thousand dollars in me to get it going." You wouldn't say, "Great. Let's go." You would investigate.

Similarly, if we really want pleasure, then we have to make sure that when we invest our most precious resources — our time and our energy — what we are pursuing is real pleasure and not counterfeit.

Comfort vs. pleasure

Among all the counterfeit pleasures that divert our efforts at true pleasure-attainment, there is one that interferes with our process more than any other.

What is the opposite experience of "pain"?

When asked this question, about nine out of ten people will answer, "Pleasure." Not only is this the wrong answer, but the belief that pleasure is the opposite of pain is, by far, the most destructive counterfeit concept that faces Western civilization! In truth, the opposite of pain is simply no pain, or comfort. And comfort is NOT at all synonymous with pleasure. Comfort is nice — it is a painless experience — but it is not pleasure, by any stretch.

In fact, pain and pleasure actually go hand in hand! Pain, or effort, is the price we pay to get pleasure. Think about it. To achieve anything in life that's really worthwhile — good relationships, successful careers, the pursuit of meaning, all of life's lasting pleasures — requires a lot of pain and effort. If you want to graduate from college so you can get a good job, you have to work hard, and sometimes study late into the night to pass your exams. If you want to keep fit so that you have the pleasure of running a marathon, you have to train; you have to experience the pain of sore muscles to attain that pleasure. If you want to be a gold-medal Olympic champion, only arduous, rigorous training will allow you to experience that incredible pleasure.

To better understand the relationship between pain and pleasure, let's return to our original example: If you ask parents what is their greatest pleasure, they are most likely to answer, "My children." If you then ask what their greatest pain is, they will probably give the very same response, "My children." It is not simply coincidental that the object of our greatest pleasure, our children, also happens to be the source of our greatest potential anguish. Pleasure and effort are far from being opposite constructs — they actually work together.

To illustrate this point, I once asked a young lady if she knew what her parents' greatest pleasure in life was.

"Sure," she told me. "Their greatest pleasure is me!"

"Of course," I said. "And what is their greatest pain?" I countered triumphantly.

"Oh, that's easy. My sister!"

She got the point. A little too well, I think.

If all you seek is comfort, it is true you'll be rid of pain, but you will also be robbed of almost any type of achievement. If you try to get at pleasure by spending your life avoiding pain, you will only end up with the world's most prominent counterfeit — comfort. Without effort, you will never get real pleasure.

In summary, to get the full pleasure available at each of level of pleasure:

- You have to become a connoisseur of that pleasure;

- You have to focus on the pleasure; and

- You have to watch out for counterfeit experiences.

Let us now examine the five different levels of pleasure.

▶ Fifth-Level Pleasure

The pleasures that are included in fifth-level pleasure are those that are most basic and most accessible to mankind — physical and material pleasure. Examples contained within this category are good food, nice clothes, comfortable furnishings and appliances, music, art, a picturesque sunset, a great car, a sweet aroma, etc.

In short, any experience that involves any of the five senses belongs in the fifth-class pleasure category. Obviously, this category is practically limitless in scope and dimension. The physical attributes of this globe are so abundant that one could never fully exhaust all the fifth-class pleasure possibilities.

Throughout time, mankind's position on physical pleasure has been as diverse as the pleasures themselves. Opinions of all extremes have always been prevalent. Western cultures, originating with Greek and Roman civilizations, have long championed the supremacy and preeminence of brute strength and ultimate comfort. Today, more than ever, hedonism rules among the masses in many societies. The ascendancy of physical pleasure as the primary goal of existence has been well documented throughout history.

On the other hand, renowned religions and many celebrated empires eschewed the worship of self-indulgence as a viable and venerated way of life. Asceticism and temperance became the respected vogue. "Life is all about restriction," they preach. "There is nothing more primitive than surrendering to your base instincts." As such, physical pleasure is looked upon with contempt and disdain.

There is, however, a third way to view physical or sensory pleasure that relates to neither extreme. And that is: physical pleasures, like all other levels of pleasurable opportunity, are Heavenly gifts to be enjoyed, like the appetizer of a really great meal. But they are clearly not the main course. The fruit cocktail or melon balls are a lovely way to whet your appetite, but never let them replace your duck à l'orange or red snapper almondine.

God did not create physical pleasures in order to frustrate you; He made them for you to enjoy. If Mom makes a new dish for dinner one night, she would be insulted if you didn't at least try it. While God does not fall prey to the clutches of personal outrage, He does expect you to, at least, taste the myriad creations that He has prepared. Of course, parameters for pleasurable experiences do call for the exclusion of unhealthy and otherwise proscribed encounters. But the Talmud (Oral Law) states that if there exists a (permissible and healthy) fruit on this earth that you have not tried, you will, one day, be called upon to explain why.

Beware...

But while you set out to explore the enormous repertoire of sensory delights, remember that each level of pleasure can be swiftly polluted by the counterfeit experiences that appear authentic, but will ultimately doom your blissful endeavor. Pursuance of physical pleasure can easily lead you down a path of self-indulgence and decadence. This occurs when it is experienced in excess. Sensory overload of any kind is neither healthy nor enjoyable.

Wine is wonderful in moderation, but guzzling down a whole bottle or two or three will probably make you violently ill and extinguish your fondness for alcohol for a good while. Salty foods may taste great, but make this your regular diet and you are likely to confront a host of unpleasant side effects.

The keys to maximizing your fifth-level pleasure are moderation and awareness.

When you partake of fifth-class pleasure without awareness, without savoring it, for the mere purpose of tantalizing your senses as an end unto itself, you will end up feeling bloated, overstuffed, and drained of energy. After that sense of immediate gratification, you are likely to feel lowered by the experience. This is not an argument for asceticism or celibacy, for these same pleasures have the potential to leave you invigorated. The key, however, to avoiding the trap of self-indulgence is awareness. When you are aware, you do not allow your appetite to rule over you. Then, you are able to maximize your fifth-class pleasure experience.

▶ Fourth-Level Pleasure

I t is clear that anyone who acquires or earns lots of money can use it to purchase a large amount of fifth-class pleasure. Twenty-five million dollars (even today) can still buy you cars, homes, vacations, and comforts galore. But if it is true that there really is no exchange rate between the pleasure levels, then fourth-class pleasure is actually worth more than $25 million or more! It is, in fact, priceless.

What is fourth-level pleasure?

Ask yourself, "What is worth more than all the physical and material pleasure in the entire world combined? What pleasure exists in the world that money just cannot buy?"

Love. Of course.

Real...genuine...bona fide love.

In this case, the Beatles were right — "Money Can't Buy You Love."

How do we know this is true?

Meet Adam Murdoch

Let's examine the fictitious case of Adam Murdoch. Adam is a rather successful investment banker in a growing Wall Street concern. He graduated summa cum laude from the University of Pennsylvania, joined the firm right out of school, and got married three years later. He's a Type "A" personality: driven, intense, ambitious...a classic workaholic. He lives in an upscale neighborhood near the Southern tip of Long Island with Amy and their two kids, drives a Toyota SUV, and recently bought a modest, but slick new boat that still awaits its maiden voyage.

Adam's goal in life is rather obvious. He wants to be a multi-millionaire...and fast. Lack of determination is not his problem. He wakes up before dawn, is drinking his third cup of coffee at his desk by 7:15, and is rarely home before the 10 p.m. news. He subscribes to over a dozen financial periodicals, most of which never get opened. He is admired by few, respected by some, and feared by many. The response he evokes from those closest to him is divided between envy and pity. Adam is "on track." But his world is about to be reeled into apprehension and angst.

He is visited one day by a man he has never met before — a representative of Paul Atwater, a renowned financier and philanthropist. After dispensing with the customary pleasantries, the gentleman explains the purpose of his encounter:

> *"I assume you are familiar with Mr. Atwater's status and reputation."*

He is. Everyone is.

> *"Mr. Atwater,"* he continues, *"has quietly been following your career from a distance. He knows your goals and aspirations and understands your approach to achieving those goals. After all, he himself was on a similar track earlier in his career, before he became affluent."*
>
> *"What's your point?"* asks Adam, nervously fumbling for his Palm. *"The foreign markets are closing in 20 minutes."*
>
> *"That is the point. Mr. Atwater would like to offer you the greatest financial short-cut of your life. You no longer have to work 60 to 70 hours a week to earn your millions. He is prepared to simply give you a cash award of $25 million. Agree to this deal and you'll never have to work again."*
>
> Adam places his Palm on the desk. *"I'm listening."*
>
> *"Mr. Atwater has everything he could possibly ever want: fortune, status, luxury, comforts people dream about. He is, however, missing just one*

thing in his life — children. He and Mrs. Atwater have longed for a child for over thirty years… but, alas, this treasured gift has been denied them. After examining many potential candidates, he concluded that you might be willing to "sell" him one of your two children for the tidy sum of $25 million.

"Now before you say no," he adds, "give it some serious thought. You leave for work before they awake. You return home after they're in bed. The little time left on weekends is spent socializing — mostly with those in line to further your career. You really never see them anyway! Why not accept this incredible offer for just one of the children? With your newfound fortune, you'll stop working, allowing your other child to finally get the father he needs!

"Besides, if you really love your child you should be concerned only for his best interest. Surely, you realize that he will be treated royally in the Atwater home. True, he might get a bit 'spoiled,' but he'll never really want for anything. And while you will not be able to ever see him again, you can take solace in knowing that you did what is truly best for him!

"Give it some thought, speak to your wife, and give me a call. Here's my card."

What is Adam's likely response to this incredible scenario?

"Holy hedge fund!! Did my ears hear right? Is he out of his mind? Does he really think that my children would be for sale?? Does Atwater think I'm some barbarian from a third-world nation who places no value on human life and relationships? What is this world coming to…"

In seconds, the man's business card would be carved into con-fetti and strewn all over the Persian rug. Even Adam understands that no amount of money, even $25 million, could induce a parent to sell a child. There is no exchange rate from fifth-class to fourth-class pleasure. The pleasure of love, of relationships, cannot be traded in for any amount of material benefit. Offended and stunned, Adam would swiftly return to his work and probably try to forget the entire absurd episode.

But in all likelihood, Adam would be unable to completely leave the events of the day behind him without being affected in some way. No matter what time he walks through his front door later that night, he is likely to tiptoe past his sleeping children, peer into their room and wonder, "I just turned down $25 million in order to keep my children. So why is it that I end up ignoring them in my quest to earn the same amount I just turned down? Those kids are obviously worth more to me than the money! And I don't even know who they are!"

A shocking realization...crystallized by a bizarre turn of events. In truth, it is a realization that we all could use, for there is a little (or a lot) of Adam in all of us.

In a flash of inspiration, Adam suddenly decides to re-order his priorities in life.

> *"I will no longer be a slave to my work," he*
> *declares triumphantly. "My days as an absentee*
> *father are over."*

He grabs one of his three cell phones and leaves a message on his secretary's voice mail:

> *Marsha, this is Adam. I won't be coming in to the*
> *office for the next two weeks. It's a long story and*
> *you wouldn't believe it anyway. Just take mes-*
> *sages and cover for me, but don't try to*
> *reach me.*
> *Thanks.*

In the morning, he shares his revelation with Amy, including his intended plan to stay at home and discover the treasures he never knew he had. After peeling Amy off the floor and supplying her with ample oxygen, Adam begins preparation on his itinerary for his newfound role as a father. He awakens the boys ever so gently, trying not to startle them too much. After all, he is a virtual stranger to them.

Within an hour, the three of them are ready for a trip to the park. A blissful day awaits them. The next 45 minutes pass as Adam struggles with the impossible task of opening the stroller — a task he had never before confronted. (And he thought commodity trading was challenging!) Eventually he surrenders and asks Amy for help. The leisurely stroll to the park then ensues. Luckily, Adam had looked up Mapquest on his laptop to get directions to the playground around the corner.

The excursion starts out innocently enough — swings, monkey bars, sandbox, etc. Adam is "bonding" as planned while resisting the urge to call the office and "log on" to his "Favorites." But fatigue strangely sets in. It's only 11:15 a.m., but our hero is exhausted. So, apparently, are the kids. And so begins the bickering, the squabbling, the complaining, belligerence, and irritation.

> *I'm thirsty.*
> *I'm tired.*
> *I don't like this park.*
> *He pushed me.*
> *It's hot!*

You get the picture. Adam is overwhelmed. He quickly learns that "reasoning" is surprisingly ineffective with toddlers. So is lecturing. He decides to change venues. After brief stints at the ice cream parlor, amusement park, and car wash, he gives up and returns home for an early dinner. He is worn-out, drained, and defeated. The kids are grumbling, fed up, and overtired.

Home-cooked dinner does little to save the day. With Amy having been set free to finally enjoy an overdue break, Adam hasn't a clue as to what they like or how to prepare it. When the meatballs start flying and simple math reveals that there is more spaghetti on the walls than in their stomachs, a "disaster" may be declared. Bedtime follows. I leave that to your imagination. Suffice it to say that by the end of the evening Adam had "Babar Goes to the Circus" committed to memory, a gallon of apple juice had been consumed or spilled, and the toilet plunger had been pressed into service more than a couple of times.

Adam collapses on the living room floor, totally spent and depleted. The clock reads 9:30 p.m. Using one final remaining gasp of energy, he clutches his trusty cell phone and dials the office.

Marsha…this is Adam. See you tomorrow.

Learning to love

What is Adam's problem? Why was the day such a disaster? Why is he cutting short his vacation by thirteen days?

Basically, Adam hasn't the slightest idea of what love really is. He has not learned how to access the pleasure of love. There's got to be more to it than just tickling your kids ad infinitum. At this point, Adam has learned one thing. His children are each worth more than $25 million. It's clear to him that the pleasure of love is priceless, but he doesn't know how to enjoy this pleasure.

Adam needs a definition. He needs to become a connoisseur of love in order to be able to appreciate it. Maimonides, a 12th-century Jewish philosopher, offers us a solid, working definition of love: **Love is the emotional pleasure a human being experiences when he understands and focuses on the virtues of another human being.**

If you do that, then even if the kids are throwing meatballs across the room, you can still love them — and discipline them at the same time. But without a clear understanding of what love is, all you'll be able to focus on is the effort and pain involved in raising kids. And there is plenty of that. In a sense, Adam is playing basketball without the ball; all he notices is the fatigue and the heat. The key to success is not eliminating the pain, that's impossible. Rather, it is to focus on the pleasure that results from all the effort.

But, as with each class of pleasure, experiencing it to its fullest usually involves some kind of price tag. On this level, you have to make the effort to really zero in on a person's virtues. Adam needs to relish his children's glee as they fly down the slide in the park. He needs to admire their creativity, even when they try to manipulate him.

Let's face it, we are all imperfect — a mixed bag of all kinds of different strengths and weaknesses. What really allows us to get into the full power of love is accepting the price tag called "commitment." When you decide to commit yourself to focus in on a person's intrinsic qualities, you will come to love him. But if all you see are the dark, threatening clouds that hover above each person, you'll rue the day you ever met him. Every moment will seem like an eternity and every encounter will make you feel distressed, angry, and guilt-ridden.

That is why we are taught in the Bible, "Love your neighbor as yourself." Isn't love a feeling? Isn't love an involuntary emotion? How can God command us to love anyone? He can do so because the decision of how we look at others is very much in our hands. The commitments we make when we choose our foci will directly determine the emotions that follow.

> "Commitment?" you say. "I'm not good at commitment. Never was. It's just not something that fits with my personality."

Perhaps that is true. But commitment happens to be a characteristic for which each of us is really wired. It's a chip that is contained within us. But for some it lays dormant — concealed behind a cloak of fear, disappointment, and painful experiences.

Let me give you an example to show you that commitment is really the key to loving and is truly accessible to all.

Ask an expectant mother or father if they are going to love the child they are about to have. What will they say?

> Of course, we are.

But don't stop there. Follow their response with one final question:

> But how do you know your child is not going to be a brat like those kids down the block that you can't stand?

Their response could be one of only two possible ones. Guaranteed.

Not my child. No kid of mine could ever become a brat. (Ignoring the fact that the real brats' parents probably felt the exact same way.)

Or:

Even if he does become a brat, we'll just love him anyway. He's our child! (Just like the parents of the real brat who, presumably, also love their obnoxious kids.)

They do not say:

Well, we'll have the child, get to know him a bit, and decide afterward, based on his personality and how cute he is, if we want to love him and keep him or not.

That would be ridiculous. As parents, they are naturally committed to loving their kids, so they do. In spite of all the deficiencies and weaknesses they observe, their love is untainted.

Age is not a factor

The commitment we have to loving our children is a given, no matter what age they are. You don't need to work at it; it comes naturally. But for any other relationship, it needs to be acquired. We need to learn how to relate to our kids and then apply those very same constructs to other relationships as well.

Imagine the following scene:

A man comes home one evening and convenes a "family meeting." When members have all gathered around the dining room table, he voices his thoughts:

"Hey! How many of you have become acquainted with the new family who moved into the corner house, the Bernsteins?"

Some have; some have not. He continues:

"Anyway, yesterday I passed their house on the way to the bakery and a ball rolled down the driveway and stopped at my feet. I reached down,

*picked it up, and tossed it to one of the Bernstein
kids in the back yard. When he caught it, instead of
resuming his game, he tossed it back to me. I guess
he thought I wanted to have a catch, or something.
I caught the ball and threw it back to him. Before
you know it, we were having a catch. I ended up
spending about 40 minutes with the Bernstein boys
and I kinda had a pretty good time!*

*"Well...one thing led to another and I found
myself in their kitchen soon after, drinking some
fresh lemonade. It was all rather innocent. But
gee whiz, those kids are really sweet!"*

*"What's the point, Dad?" ask his growingly
impatient children.*

*"Well...I don't really know what to say. I guess
it's kinda hard to tell you this, but I think I have
fallen in love with the Bernstein kids. So, starting
this weekend, you guys are out and they are in!"*

Admittedly, this scenario is rather preposterous. Even in the
insane, bizarre world in which we live today, you don't find
people falling madly in love with other people's children. It's
not normal. But marriages fall apart every day for the very
same reason. Is it logical? Why is it more reasonable to break up
with one's spouse than with one's children? Truth be told, our
spouses are the ones we chose to marry, while our children are
accidents of birth! Why don't we find more divorces between
parent and child?

The answer, of course, is commitment. The commitment to
love between parent and child is natural, but it has to be earned
between husband and wife.

And the commitment to loving our children doesn't really
change, even when they are grown up. That's how powerful this
dynamic is. In fact, the unalterable status of this feeling state is
so steadfast that it is almost totally independent of what actions
our children may perpetrate.

Tens of thousands of people, all over the world, commit a vast
range of cruel and unspeakable crimes. But when the parents of

these people are questioned as to whether they still love their children, the responses invariably confirm that nothing could alter their feelings. Episodes as ghastly as rape or mass murder are summarily dismissed as resulting from "hanging around with the wrong crowd," or "I guess he had a bad day." But rarely could any experience ever really contaminate the ironclad commitment that binds the parent-child relationship.

Infatuation — the counterfeit

Remember, enjoying each level of pleasure takes more than just finding the remote control and flicking a switch. You've got to define the available pleasures (become a connoisseur) and focus away from the effort. But you also have to steer clear of the counterfeit experience. The counterfeit experience of fifth-level (physical) pleasure, you may recall, is sensory overload. The counterfeit of fourth-level pleasure is infatuation.

Let's face it. Man has always looked for short-cuts, and why not? Many short-cuts are brilliant timesaving and energy-saving creations. But as technological advances become more and more sweeping, we find ourselves less and less willing to wait and/or work for anything. It stands to reason that in this instant world of ours, love would be no exception. Why work for it when we can just "fall" in love? After all, where would every great love story and motion picture be without this magical and mythical concept?

I'll tell it to you straight. You may disagree. You may hate me for it. But the concept that love is not something you choose, but rather something that just "happens" to you, is a lie — a beautiful, romantic, extremely popular, fabulously alluring lie. In short, Cupid is duping the world. And most of us fall for it.

Oh, don't get me wrong. It is very possible to be instantly attracted to someone, or fascinated by a person's wit, charisma, or intellect. Happens all the time. And those responses in you should not be ignored. They may be great signals that this is someone you should get to know better. Absolutely. But real love is much more than that. Real love requires a careful evaluation of whether, in fact, this person's understanding, perceptions, goals, and lifestyles really do jibe with yours. That process takes time, effort, and honest scrutiny.

It's not as cold and calculated as it sounds. There's plenty of room for the warm and fuzzy emotions that get summoned up inside of you. After all, that's what probably got you interested in the first place! But chances are that if you "fall" in love, sooner or later you will also "fall" out of love. That's why they say, "Love is blind." The real truth is, "Infatuation is blind." Love is more like a magnifying glass that allows you to see the other person in his entirety — examining every aspect of the strengths and weak-nesses, personal value system, and unique personality that forge a human being.

There is no such thing as effort-free loving. This is a counter-feit; this is infatuation and lust. Real, committed love is forever.

So how do you know if you are in love or just infatuated? If you ever catch yourself saying, "He's perfect," or, "She's perfect," then beware! That is not reality. The mirage of perfection is a sure sign of infatuation.

Real love takes work. If you want that pleasure, it's available within every relationship. But you have to be willing to make the effort.

Good luck!

▶ Third-Level Pleasure

Throughout history, there have been many periods when man was obsessed with the accumulation of wealth and physical (fifth-level) pleasures. The U.S.A. has long been an acknowledged world leader in this particular fascination. We just can't seem to get enough fifth-level pleasure.

There have also been times — the '60's for example — when "love" (fourth-level pleasure) or infatuation (its counterfeit) seemed to rule the planet, or, at least, the country. Love "com-munes" sprung up everywhere. Nearly every communication the media transmitted seemed to smack, in some way, of the "love" message.

But, sooner or later, people often realize that there may be more to life than money and love. There is something deeper — a pleasure even more satisfying in the world, that when we meet up with it, we realize intuitively that we have reached a different, more rewarding station in life.

That is the pleasure of meaning — doing something that is good and meaningful in some way. This is third-level pleasure.

According to our model, we have asserted that there is no exchange rate between the classes of pleasure. The people we truly love are truly priceless. No money in the world could convince us to give up that pleasure. The question now is: What pleasure exists that would actually compel us to give up what we love, in order to attain it? The answer, it seems, is meaning.

It is hard to imagine someone actually sacrificing the immense pleasure derived from a child, a loving spouse or friend, or a parent, for any reason whatsoever, and yet it happens all the time.

Earlier we met Adam Murdoch — driven, industrious, determined, yet still unwilling to "sell" his children. Certainly any parent would feel the same way. But what if Adam or Mrs. Murdoch, or you, for that matter, had a meaningful cause — a cause that you really lived for — that might also be a cause for which you would even die? People voluntarily sacrifice, suffer, and yes, even die, for religious or humanitarian freedoms or in wars for independence. Nothing strange or unusual about it at all. If the cause is meaningful enough, we would all be ready and willing to surrender huge amounts of pleasurable experiences and potential, perhaps even our lives, in order to take part in it. Our own lives and the lives of our very own children would swiftly become comparatively insignificant in our quest for meaning. In the immortal words of our 6th-grade social studies texts when quoting American patriot Nathan Hale, "My only regret is that I have but one life to give for my country."

"It's so hard..."

We can all see that doing the "right thing" can bring us colossal units of pleasure. We worship the hero and heroine as they sacrifice "everything they've got" just to affirm their principles and actualize their beliefs. We root for them to succeed and we pray that "good" will triumph over "evil." But for us, doing the "right" thing is not so easy. We become blind to the pleasure potential inherent in meaningful pursuits and instead see only the effort involved.

There's no hiding it. It takes enormous effort to be a genuinely good person. Truthfully? Most people never reach this goal. They end up being "not bad" — that is, they don't murder anybody, they don't steal or commit heinous felonies. Of course, not doing anything "really bad" is not so grand after all, is it? People who are tragically in comas don't do anything "bad" either. No. Being "good" is much more than just not being bad. But the effort involved in being truly good is so intense that it usually prevents us from really trying.

And yet, it is something we all really desire.

Read the obituary page of any newspaper. Carefully review the descriptions of the lives of the deceased. The commonalities are rather obvious. Every description summarizes the person's accomplishments in life. The only thing that seems to matter "in the end" is how many Boards he served on, how much charity he gave, and his overall contribution to his community or society at large. I have yet to read an obituary that lionizes someone's monetary accruals.

> ...Mr. Werthington was 86 years old. He owned a
> 98-foot yacht, dined only in the finest restaurants,
> and never paid less than $1200 for a suit.

Ridiculous.

Being "good" — it's powerful!

The power of doing something "good" is easily recognized. When we examine even a very minor "good" deed, the power we feel is palpable.

Take, for example, a simple retail transaction. Most of us make many such deals every week. Often, the clerk involved is required to give a certain amount of change. Occasionally, the clerk makes an error and gives an incorrect amount of change.

We usually count the change and alert him to the oversight. It happens every day.

But sometimes the clerk gives us too much change. If you have ever experienced the thrill of returning the extra change to the clerk, you know how good it feels, even if the amount was a trivial quarter or a nickel! Somehow, the "goodness" of the deed transcends the actual magnitude of the error. Being virtuous, even for a nickel, just feels great.

Now, let's zero in on that great feeling. The clarity with which we emerge can help us understand why doing meaningful acts eludes us so frequently.

Imagine the following two scenes:

Scene #1

You are sitting on a park bench one summer afternoon. A gentleman walks past you and an envelope falls from his pocket.

"Sir," you call out, "you dropped something."

The fellow looks down and retrieves the envelope.

"Thank you, thank you, thank you," he joyously sings. "You don't know what you did for me!"

He shows you the envelope. Inside is $100,000 in cash. The man just came from the bank and was on his way to make a down payment on his "dream" house. He embraces you, hands you a $1 reward, and goes on his way.

Scene #2

You are sitting alone on a park bench. You look down at your feet and notice an envelope. You pick it up, look inside and find $100,000 in cash. Incredible! And yet, these things have actually happened, just not to you. What do you do? You look around; no one is within sight. If you are especially righteous, you say to yourself, "There's no way I can keep this. I'll wait around. Surely the owner will come. The disappearance of this amount of money will be quickly noticed. But I'm not going to wait all day. I'll wait...say...uh...30 minutes. After that...well, it's mine. I can live with that."

Anxiously you begin the countdown. Sweat slowly saturates your body. Each minute feels like an eternity. Ten, 20, 25, 29 minutes go by — no one has arrived. But then...in the distance, you discern a man dashing frantically up the path. Out of breath and in total disarray, he approaches you.

> *"I dropped an envelope near here. It's extremely valuable. Did you by any chance, see it?"*

Resignation sets in. You're in shock. You reach into your breast pocket and remove the envelope.

> *"What is in the envelope?" you inquire indignantly.*
> *"$100,000 – all in 50's," comes the dreaded and correct answer.*

Handing over the envelope, you mutter something inaudible about being more careful, turn around, and shuffle your way home.

Two similar scenes with great contrasts. In both scenes, the same amount of money is returned, but clearly, the circumstances are vastly different. In the first scene, you are the catalyst in getting the money back to its rightful owner, but you have no idea what is in the envelope when you return it. In the second scene, you are fully aware of what you are doing.

There can be no doubt that the selfless act in the second scene is far more meritorious than the simple lost and found episode of the first scene. But there can also be no doubt that at the moment in scene 2 when the money is actually returned, you're feeling a lot more pain and ambivalence than in scene 1! How could that be? Didn't we just conclude that doing something really meaningful is a wonderfully pleasurable experience? And isn't there far more meaning in scene 2 than in scene 1?

The answer to these questions is critical to understanding the elusiveness of third-level pleasure, as well as its potency.

In scene 1, you had no conflict whatsoever. Not knowing the contents of the envelope, you played Good Samaritan and directed the envelope to its rightful owner. Period. No reason not to feel great.

But the pleasures available to you in Scene 2 are impeded by the fact that you were already depositing the money into your account when the guy showed up! The immense pleasure of discounting your own fortune and returning the money is absolutely staggering! But it cannot become available to you immediately. There is too much conflict hindering the process. There's usually heaps of effort, ambivalence, and even pain involved in doing something really meaningful. Only in the future, when the exertion has ended and faded away, will you be able to look back and fully appreciate and enjoy what you did. Then the retroactive pleasure will be truly astounding.

Let's get practical

Of course, just knowing intellectually that immense satisfaction awaits us "somewhere down the road" is frequently not sufficient motivation to get us to do something meaningful right now. We've become accustomed to instant gratification, so we want the pleasure NOW! We must learn how to appreciate third-class pleasure in a more immediate sense.

One way of doing that is to sit down at the end of every day, when the effort of what you've done is behind you, and focus your attention on what you did that was good and meaningful. Five or 10 minutes should be sufficient. The more you practice that, the more you will become a connoisseur of being good, and eventually you will be able to get some of the pleasure even while you're "under siege."

Another way to develop the skill of appreciating third-class pleasure is to seriously consider what you are willing to dedicate yourself to. What does this mean? From our discussion thus far, it is clear that there are certain causes, principles, or ideals for which we might actually be willing to die. But, the question arises: How many of us are also willing to live for the same cause? If America or your homeland were attacked, you might rush to the front lines to defend it. But in your everyday life, you focus on your own insular world without considering this cause in the least. Maybe you will give a few dollars to a charity related to the cause, or maybe on Election Day you will show up to vote. Nonetheless, through the daily grind of living, we are not really in touch with those issues that do, in fact, matter deeply to us.

To become a real connoisseur of third-class pleasure, you first need to know what you would be willing to die for. Until then, you haven't fully begun living!

More importantly, though, once you have identified this source of meaning and pleasure, you need to know whether you are willing to live for it as well. The connoisseur of third-class pleasure knows what he or she is living for. Until you find that cause, all you are chasing is fifth-class and fourth-class pleasure. You are not living life to the hilt. Third-class pleasure soars above the other two levels. Attaining it gives you value, self-respect, and genuine purpose in life.

If you don't have meaning in your life, the other pleasures can become "so what" pleasures. All the physical trappings, the beautiful vacations, and even the wonderful spouse and children, can make you feel that something is still missing. Again, if you are not living today in accordance with the causes, principles, or ideals for which you are willing to die, you are not really living much at all.

Shocked into reality

Everyone knows about the Nobel Prize. Alfred Nobel, wealthy Swedish industrialist, decided one day to honor life's greatest achievers. Outstanding physicists, economists, authors, and scores of other eminent personalities are honored periodically and receive worldwide acclaim for their contributions to society. But few people know the genesis of this coveted award program. What really motivated Alfred Nobel to establish this most sought-after prize?

Nobel was best known as the inventor of dynamite in 1866. One day, Nobel's brother died. The local newspaper mistakenly thought that Nobel himself had died and they wrote an obituary about him. Nobel actually had the unfortunate, or rather, the fortunate experience of doing something very few people ever do. He read his own obituary. Imagine his shock as he read that his main accomplishment in life was being responsible for vast destruction in the world. Seeing it in print made his life's work seem worthless at best and brutal at worst. It was this staggering jolt that triggered Nobel to found the Nobel Prize.

When you dare to come face to face with your truest beliefs and ideals, and ask yourself the really important questions about what you want your obituary to look like, the effect is remarkable.

The counterfeit lurks...

However, in your search for meaning, you have to be very careful. It is so easy to fall for the counterfeit. Since the effort involved in procuring bona fide third-class pleasure is so great, the counterfeit seems all the more enticing. In this class of pleasure, the counterfeit of being good is "looking good." And if you do not know what genuine good really is, then you are likely to be expending a lot of effort trying to win the admiration of your peers and society in order to make yourself feel important. Let's be honest. *Looking* important is so much easier than *being* important.

The most prevalent counterfeit coin for "good" in Western society is being a financial success. If you are not financially successful, you can be a good husband, a good friend, and a loyal, decent citizen, but you are still a failure. The power of money seems to be infinite, even though on some level everybody knows that there are scores of people out there who simultaneously are rich, famous, and also the lowest dregs on the planet. The list of these pitiable souls is rather extensive, but somehow, most of us cannot shake the notion that if we have not succeeded financially, we just haven't made it in life.

Ever wonder why so many of these superficial glamour gods — people with huge mansions and gardens, yachts, and wardrobes ad infinitum, whose children go to the "best" schools, still drift from marriage to marriage, and from drug to drug, or even end it all? Don't these people have everything? The fact is that the pleasures in their lives do not offer the essential meaning they are seeking and need so desperately. Therefore, as they acquire more and more fifth- and fourth-class pleasures, they feel emptier and emptier, because they do not know how to get that which they truly crave.

Don't fall for just looking good. Deeds are the genuine articles, and ultimately, they will provide you with the self-respect for which you really long. It is a basic energy that we all require. After all, without self-respect we have nothing.

There was an incident some years ago where a Brink's delivery truck lost several bags of money, millions of dollars. It seems the back door flew open and the bags tumbled into the street, the money scattering in the wind. Passersby grabbed as much as they could. Out of $4 million, only $50,000 was recovered. A day or two later a fellow walked into the bank and returned the money he had found. The press gave it big play; this was something really newsworthy! What a guy!

But when they interviewed his father, his reaction was anything but proud.

"My son is a wimp," he cried!

His fellow workers voiced similar sentiments.

"God gave him a gift and the idiot gave it back,"
was the prevailing refrain.

We can hardly imagine the effort and the pain involved in the decision to return the money. If he had kept the money, he could have bought (temporary) success. ($50,000 doesn't take you too far anymore.) But the price tag of that fleeting achievement would have been theft. No small price to pay. Instead, he acquired authentic, unadulterated, long-lasting third-class pleasure.

It is the real thing.

WARNING: IF YOU ARE SATISFIED WITH ATTAINING FIFTH-, FOURTH-, AND THIRD-LEVELS OF PLEASURE, AND BEING A "GOOD" PERSON, STOP HERE! DO NOT READ FURTHER UNLESS YOU WANT TO BE A "GREAT" PERSON!

▸ Second-Level Pleasure

It's clear to see how mastering third-class pleasure will make you a good person. But it's second-class pleasure that can really make you great. And the difference between "good" and "great" is vast.

In order to best understand the power and the subtleties of second-class pleasure, let's take a little "field trip" to a neighborhood construction site and speak to three seasoned construction workers on the job.

Worker number one seems to be intensely involved in his work. His muscles glisten in the sunlight and he handles the jackhammer like Barry Bonds wielding a plastic baseball bat. So focused is he on the demolition mission to which he is assigned that he hardly notices us approaching.

> *"Pardon me, sir, we're conducting a little survey today. I was wondering if you could help us."*
>
> *"Sure."*
>
> *"You seem to really love your work. Why is that? And why are you here today?"*
>
> *"Well, you couldn't be more correct. You see these biceps and triceps? Amazing, aren't they? Well, this doesn't happen from being a toll collector or an accountant. You want a really great body, you gotta work for it. And construction is the perfect way of earning a few bucks while building your bulk. I get to work and work out, at the same time. Got it?"*
>
> *"Sure...thanks!"*

Let's move on now to worker number two.

> *"Sir...why are you here?"*
>
> *"Well, I've been in this line of work for over twenty years, so I've got a pretty good salary package. And I've got a wife and three kids at home. Truth is, they are my whole life. They deserve the best and this job allows me to give it to them. You know...not just food on the table, but the little extras that make life special. That's why I'm here."*
>
> *"Good explanation and good luck to you!"*

Let's turn now to worker number three and find out why he is at this site.

"That's a really good question because the truth is, I could pretty much name my assignment. I've got lots of seniority in this business and the foreman asked me where I wanted to work next.

"I chose this site because we are building the first hospital in this town. I'm tired of building apartment houses, stadiums, and bowling alleys, and for years the citizens here have been without a major medical facility. When I heard they were finally building a hospital I knew I wanted to be a part of it. One day when this building is finished, I will drive by with my grandkids and tell them, 'I built this place.' That's why I'm here."

"Beautiful. Lots of luck to you."

Three construction workers, all here for very different reasons. Worker number one uses this occupation as a way to build his physique. He is getting fifth-level pleasure. Worker number two is dedicated to his family. His labor is a labor of love. He is getting fourth-level pleasure. And worker number three chose this assignment because of the significance of the project. Building a hospital could certainly be considered third-level pleasure.

But there is someone, totally absent from this scene, who is probably getting more pleasure than all of these people. He is someone who operates on a different level of foresight and meaning. Who is that?

It could be the architect. He designed the building.

It could also be the members of the committee, whose vision it was to build the hospital in the first place. Or the fundraisers, who actually saw to it that this hospital could be a viable project. Or the philanthropists who really made this undertaking a reality. Their level of satisfaction and fulfillment far exceeds that of the construction workers.

They are all getting second-level pleasure — the pleasure of creativity. When they drive by this building, they will tell their grandchildren, "I built this place." How true it will be.

However...

Being able to utilize our creative abilities is truly an enormous pleasure, but if the achievement were only creative, without also being meaningful, the experience would not qualify as a second-level pleasure. Writing music or poetry, or designing a park or a dress, certainly is a creative process, but unless those creations have meaning attached to them, the process is not more than a fifth-level pleasure. So level two is inexorably connected to level three. It is an extension of third-level pleasure that attaches a new dimension to our role in a meaningful process, which can even affect the world.

Similarly, every soldier in every significant battle can, given the appropriate time frame, take great third-level pleasure in his efforts. It is a huge responsibility and the rewards are commensurate with the effort. But the officers, especially the generals, who actually plan the military strategy that is operationalized on the front, have the potential to also experience second-level pleasure — being creative in a meaningful way.

But you don't have to be a renowned philanthropist or a brilliant general to avail yourself of this incredible class of pleasure and satisfaction. Don't think that only unusually gifted and creatively talented people ever reach the second-level summit. Not so. That definition would severely limit the pool of those who are capable of accessing this nearly incomparable life experience.

Every time you offer advice to a friend that helps him out of a tough spot, you encounter second-level pleasure. Every time you sit in a meeting, at work, in your community, or with friends, and the group decides to implement your idea, you are touching second-level pleasure. Teaching, whether professionally or informally, is a great manifestation of your creative capacities, and is second-level pleasure. And one of the greatest examples of second-level pleasure is creating a family — not just giving birth, but inculcating family members with values and character traits that will make them happy and contributing members of society.

Creativity...from where does it come?

Now, some people are just more creative than others. This is true. Perhaps they were born that way, being innately more creative. Very possible. But the real secret to becoming more creative is increasing your understanding of the world around you. The more you understand, the more you can create. You actually draw from your well of perception and insight to generate and craft new ideas and the ways to communicate them best. And that well is composed of knowledge, experience, and understanding. For that you need to study, keep your eyes and ears open, and ask questions! Yes, even stupid ones. That's how your brain expands and develops this most pleasurable skill.

Without keen insight into what is important and potentially most pleasurable (in a true sense), you can win $100 million in a lottery and be a totally miserable person. In fact, it is well documented that this is exactly what does happen to most lottery winners! Lacking genuine understanding of the world, they squander their fortune, make scores of enemies, and end up more depressed and aimless than they were before.

But with real appreciation of life's priorities and potential (and with a clear understanding of the five levels of pleasure), you could live with not much more than your basic necessities and be a totally fulfilled and content person. The key is understanding.

The counterfeit

World history is replete with individuals who were saturated with abundantly creative skills. Many were creative in ways that were not particularly meaningful, while many used their distinctive gifts to help shape a better world. But there were also those who used their unique abilities for one reason and one reason only — power.

The Stalins, Hitlers, and Saddam Husseins of the world possessed enormous capacity to create. Unfortunately, they were only interested in their own power. They used their talents to control and manipulate those around them for the sole purpose of gaining influence and establishing supremacy. This is the counterfeit experience of second-class pleasure.

Tyrants of this ilk will disregard all rules of society and even forego all other forms of pleasure, just to get a nibble of this poisonous elixir called "power." All the while, millions of lives are sacrificed toward this perverted and twisted ideal. Bona fide second-class pleasure is the power to create life, not destroy it.

But those falling prey to counterfeit second-level pleasure are not limited to dictators and despots. The lure of power is so great and the trap so intoxicating that it can actually affect all of us in ways we cannot imagine. People often make the mistake of thinking that simple control or manipulation makes them creative; they see this control as an end in itself, and that is the inherent danger.

Imposing our ideas on others, regardless of their actual worth, is an all too common counterfeit experience. An employer who wields the supremacy of his position just to satisfy his lust for control is guilty of a common societal malady, and of chasing second-class counterfeit pleasure. Even those of us who can "never be wrong" also unwittingly suffer from the pursuance of second-class counterfeit. Stalin, Hitler, and Idi Amin are extreme examples of those duped by this illusion, but everyone is really in danger of yielding to this most enticing sensation.

The way to tell if you are really creating or just controlling is by looking at the result: creativity gives pleasure to the creator and to others around him, whereas control leads only to destruction and misery.

In conclusion...

As you can see, defining creativity and its accompanying pleasure is no simple feat. The thrill you get when you formulate a solution to a troubling state of affairs is difficult to describe. We know the excitement we feel when our idea is voted in, and yet its components are elusive. Why do we feel the way we do? What is it about creativity that packs so much pleasure?

The answer may be that creativity actually touches the essence of God Himself. After all, creativity is what defines God, beginning with the universe around us and everything else that followed. Only a Supreme Being can create ex nihilo, something from nothing, but when we use our "Divine spark" to formulate a new concept, idea, or methodology, we too are nearly Godlike. Expressing our own creativity is but a taste of His power. No wonder, then, that its complete definition defies full clarity. You see, emulating our Creator is a pleasure that really has no equal...as we are about to see in first-level pleasure.

▸ First-Level Pleasure

We have finally reached first-level pleasure — the "zenith" of our model for attaining maximum pleasure on this planet and living life to the fullest. If money were no object, everyone would certainly want to travel first class, no matter where he was going. How about the journey we call "life"? What exactly is first-class pleasure...in life?

Earlier in our paradigm, we "visited" several different locations: a basketball yard, the Murdoch home on Long Island, a park bench, and a construction site. Let's take one final trip now, in the hopes of clarifying the full impact of first-level pleasure.

Come and join me for a field trip to the local Public Library. Let's go to the "Fiction" section and find the shelves where the books of Stephen King are kept. As you know, Stephen King is a very popular author, and while we have chosen him for our illustration, the same point can be made with any well-liked author who has had many books published over the years.

Let's remove a copy of each of King's novels and place them, face up, on a nearby table, so we can see them all in one blush. We now have approximately twenty-nine books on the table.

Allow me to propose to you the following challenge. Pretend for the moment that you have never heard of Stephen King and have certainly never read or even heard of any of his books.

Without opening or even touching the books, try to place them in the correct sequence in which they were published. Given that the books were all in mint condition, would you be able to put them in proper order? Could you come close?

Not so easy.

Even if you knew that his first book, "Carrie," was written in 1974, that wouldn't help you much, would it?

How is it possible to guess the approximate order of publishing without knowing anything about the books?

Here is the answer.

Marketing.

That's right...marketing. You see, when King or any author has his first novel published, he is an unknown quantity. The publishing house knows this and directs the folks over at "cover design" to feature the book's title in big, bold letters. The author's name appears in relatively small print. But as he becomes more and more popular, the marketing department realizes they have a star on their hands. They understand that people are now buying the author, not the book.

> *Excuse me, sir; do you have the new Stephen King book in stock?*

What it is called is comparatively insignificant. So by the time the year 2001 rolls around and Stephen King has sold a zillion books in his career, his newest title, "Dreamcatcher," is featured in a smaller font. "Stephen King" is emblazoned in large front-cover letters. That's the secret in placing the books in approximate sequence; the title is getting smaller, while the author is getting larger.

Welcome to first-level pleasure

First-level pleasure occurs when you experience the awe of the Author of the world, God Himself. You can go through life, day-by-day, and just see the "titles" of the world, or you can live your life on a totally different plane and focus only on the "Author" of all of life's experiences. Every object, every experience, every relationship, thought, and feeling can be seen in the mundane or can be seen as a "holy" creation — the fingerprint of God. When you do that, when you tap into the awesome power and unique qualities of everything around you, you see God, the "Author." You begin to really understand your purpose and the purpose of creation. Life on that transcendental sphere is absolutely, positively, utterly, and completely...first class!

Human beings have always had a drive for the ultimate experience. For some, it has been the pursuit of immortality, the "Fountain of Youth." For others it is the quest for the "Holy Grail," "eternal bliss," or even "The Wizard of Oz." Some describe the yearning as "spiritual" or "religious," while others refer to the longing as just "IT!" But no matter what nebulous terminology is used to describe the search, it is clear that each one of us, deep down, has a desire to reach out beyond ourselves, beyond our own finite world, and to touch the infinite. No human being is totally satisfied unless he has at least touched the ultimate experience. That is what we are seeking — to somehow sense the interconnectedness of all existence, to touch the transcendental.

And what, pray tell, is that?

Imagine if I said, "I know a place where you can go and actually speak with God Himself. You can sit down, meet Him, and ask Him anything you like for an hour." Would we not all agree that that would be the "It" experience? That connection with God is the enchanted elixir we all seek to drink.

Now, this notion may sound vague and fluffy, but it is not nearly as improbable as it seems. Fact is, we have all had moments when we have been struck by the awesomeness of life — whether it's watching sunrise from a mountain summit, witnessing the birth of a newborn, experiencing the vastness of the galaxies, or encountering a raging storm or volcano — we have all experienced something in life that takes our breath away. Those are moments that are filled with awe.

Now, defining what "awe" actually is can be rather daunting. But perhaps it can be said that awe is the experience we feel when we merge our small, relatively speaking, insignificant selves with something that is much greater than us. We break beyond our own limitations and touch something far more complex than ourselves...something truly unlimited and immeasurable. It is then that we feel connected to the unity of God.

This first-class pleasure is categorically above everything else; it is the drive for ultimate meaning — to sense who you are in the great scheme of things and to know that that place transcends the finite moment. That is the greatest pleasure available to us!!

Sure...but how much does it cost?

By now, you should be well versed in how this process works. As on all the other levels, here too there is a price to pay. And it stands to reason that for first-class pleasure, that price might be pretty steep. It is. Here, the price tag is called "gratitude."

In order to really connect with God, you have to learn to appreciate all the good He has done for you. That means giving up the illusion that you alone are responsible for your achievements, and admitting that whatever you have is truly a gift from God. Just as every stroke of Picasso's brush has his signature on it, everything in this world has God's signature on it. You just have to learn to appreciate it.

And why is this awareness so difficult to attain and sustain? Because a human being's ego always craves recognition and independence. It balks at the concept of indebtedness to a Higher Power. We prefer to believe we've done it ourselves. To develop this brand of humility takes real effort and focus.

However, if you do make the effort to appreciate all the gifts God has bestowed upon you, then you'll have such a keen awareness of God's presence that everything you do will be literally saturated by His love and guidance. You'll be overwhelmed above and beyond any other pleasure possible.

This, by the way, is where service to the Almighty fits in as well. So much of daily life revolves around service to God: whether through prayer, fulfilling commandments, or tradition. Unfortunately, many are prone to experience this service as obligatory, routine, or even oppressive. And the results of these attitudes are usually disastrous. More often than not, this mind-set yields conduct that is ceremonious, at best, and resentful, at worst.

But when service is conducted as a consequence of feelings of true gratitude and love, the man/God connection is lofty, energizing, and exhilarating.

In fact, this is the ultimate goal for which man was created. We were put on earth in order to overcome the illusions and use our free will to build a relationship with God. He could have made robots, but God doesn't want that. He wants a real relationship — which means we have to choose it.

The inevitable counterfeit

The counterfeit experience at this level is arrogance and self-absorption.

Arrogance and the obsession with self create the false impression of the ultimate experience. Just as only humility will enable you to transcend your ego in order for you to perceive your greater self in the scheme of all of reality, so does its opposite "promise" to bring you to the same end. To see yourself as "all-powerful," in "total control," and as B.M.O.C. (Big Man on Campus) is a tremendous high, a high which seems totally complete. It is, however, a high that leaves no room for anything outside yourself, and you are left with nowhere to transcend to. Like all counterfeits, it is just an illusion, which will eventually crumble.

Let's end with a story...

A man was interested in the phenomenon of the Chassidic Rebbe. A Chassidic Rebbe is a man who inherited the title or was chosen as the leader of his particular Judaic sect. All Chassidic Rebbes follow the same basic laws, practices, and traditions, but some customs vary depending on the history of the European town in which the sect originated.

One day, the man paid a visit to the headquarters of such a Rebbe in order to observe his daily routine. A portion of the leader's day is often spent attending to the particular needs of his constituents. People come, they wait their turn, and eventually get to speak to the Rebbe and receive his advice and sage counsel on a variety of topics ranging from health and business to spiritual growth and family matters.

Today, this fellow spends several hours on his "research" trip, observing the scores of interviews and noting the protocols and methodology of the Rebbe. At the end of the day, the man has completed his observations and approaches the Rebbe with this surprising and brazen statement:

> *"Rebbe, I thank you for this opportunity today, but frankly speaking, I fail to see the unique qualities that one must possess in order to qualify to be a Rebbe. People come, you greet them politely. They speak, you listen. Sometimes you offer them some common sense advice. Occasionally you share a cold drink or a fruit. What's the 'big deal' about being a Rebbe? I think I could do a pretty good job myself!"*

The Rebbe hears the question, strokes his beard pensively, and responds convincingly:

> *"You make a good point. From what you actually witness, there seems to be no distinctive or inherently special qualities to being a Rebbe. But I will tell you the real difference between you and me.*
>
> *"When you leave this building today, you will likely make a left turn, walk down the block, and pass the beautiful apple tree on the corner. Upon seeing that tree you might look up admiringly and say to yourself, 'Look at this exquisite tree with luscious apples. I must have one of these apples.' You reach up, pluck an apple from its branch, recite the appropriate blessing, and eat the apple.*
>
> *"When I leave the building," says the Rebbe, "I too will make a left turn, walk down the block, and pass the beautiful apple tree on the corner. I will look up admiringly and say to myself, 'Look at this exquisite tree with luscious apples. I must...say a blessing.' Whereupon I will reach up, pluck an*

apple from its branch, recite the blessing, and eat the apple.

"To the untrained eye, the actions of the two of us will be exactly the same. The difference is that you say the blessing in order to eat the apple. I am eating the apple only in order to say the blessing."

The lesson is clear. When someone like the Rebbe is focused solely on first-class pleasure, then he sees God's hand in everything around him. If not, all you get is fifth-class pleasure. And THAT is a huge difference. Even eating an apple can be a fifth-class pleasure or a first-class pleasure. It all depends on your perspective.

The wrap-up

Know this:

We were all created to have pleasure. The trick is:

• Don't get fooled by the counterfeit;

• Know what the real pleasures are; and

• Don't be afraid of the effort.

It takes hard work to become an Olympic champion, but it takes even harder work to become a champion human being!

This world is a repository of endless opportunities for pleasure. Is there a lot of pain and suffering out there too? Sure. But our job is to focus our attention on the good stuff. Five different levels of it. Each one is chock full of incredible prospects for ultimate enjoyment.

All categories are important. But don't settle for comfort or the lower levels of pleasure only. Go for the gold!

You'll be glad you did.

2 PRAYER

Question: Does anything more pure exist on this planet than the sight of a young child praying fervently and sincerely in a time of need?

Answer: No.

t is hard to imagine something more wholesome than a child's prayer. And so, the story is told of a young girl, perhaps 10 years old, who was seen praying intently at the synagogue one Saturday. Services were winding down and the assembled began their exit from the sanctuary, but this young maiden lingered on — swaying, praying, and beseeching the Almighty for mercy of some kind.

A gentleman caught a glimpse of this most unusual display of sincerity and passion and decided to inquire as to her plea and purpose. It was a good 10 minutes before the young lady finally emerged.

"Pardon me," he began, "I couldn't help notice how beautifully you were praying. Do you mind if I ask what it was you were praying for so strongly?"

"Well...I'm a little embarrassed that you saw me," she answered, "but my birthday is coming up this week." Her eyes widened as she spoke. "I could sure use a new bike!"

"Oh...I see. I'm sorry to embarrass you, but I do wish you Happy Birthday and lots of luck!"

The gentleman and the girl parted ways, but bumped into each other on the street about two weeks later.

"Hey," said the man, "aren't you the birthday girl I met a couple of weeks ago?"

"Yes, I remember you," she said.

"Tell me," he continued, "were your prayers answered?"

"As a matter of fact they were," she told him.

"How wonderful!" proclaimed the man. "Are you enjoying your brand-new bike?"

"Well...I didn't actually get a new bike," she admitted.

"What? I thought you said your prayers were answered!"

"They were," said the girl. "The answer was, 'No.'"

People pray.

Some pray every day, some pray five times a day. Some pray once a week, some pray only when they "really" have to.

Some pray silently, some pray out loud.

They pray in synagogues and in churches, and in foxholes of all shapes, sizes, and predicaments.

But everyone hopes that his prayers will be answered.

And they are.

Sometimes the answer is "Yes," and sometimes it is "No."

When our prayers are answered in the affirmative, it is quite obvious that we have been answered. But when the answer is "No," most of us fail to recognize that the denial of our request is also an answer. Conclusion? God listens and He responds.

Of course, we would all like to find the key, the secret to getting the "Yes" response whenever it is possible. Naturally, guaranteeing that we get that answer is rather impossible, but that does not mean that we can't "stack the deck," use every possible tool to try to gain the upper hand, so to speak, and "influence" God's choices when He decides how to answer our prayers.

But before we do that, a few words are necessary about what prayer is really all about and to Whom it is we are praying.

Prayer — for Him or for us?

If we really want prayer to "work," it makes sense to understand how this concept we call "prayer" actually works. It is shocking how many people have the wrong idea of the purpose and the mechanics of prayer.

For most people, prayer is either a laundry list of requests to "remind" Him of what it is we need most (absurd), or a "wake-up call" to God to let Him know that we need some help down here (beyond absurd). After all, what could be more ridiculous than praying to a God Who we obviously think can hear us and provide for our every need — big and small — while simultaneously thinking that He needs us to inform Him that His assistance and intervention might be useful for a while? And yet that is what prayer ends up being for so many of us!

We would do well to remember two major points about God and our relationship with Him.

We are praying to a Being that is, at the same time, All-Knowing, All-Powerful, and All-Loving. There is nothing in this universe, not a ripple in a creek, not a chirp of a sparrow, not a chip of a processor, or a whimper of a baby, that He did not create. For although it is man who invents and manufactures products, it is God Who implants in man the wisdom to do so. When Abraham, the first human to recognize the existence of one God, brought the concept of monotheism into reality, his declaration of the "Oneness" of God meant not only that there was "One God" and not two, but also that His Unity meant there was nothing in existence beyond His scope and command. From crocodiles to cashew nuts, and from imagination to photography, God made it all.

Does He really need your reminders of what you think you need?

Not only is God eminently capable of knowing and providing for your every need, but, more importantly, He also wants to give those things to you even more than you want them yourself! That is precisely why He created you. That is what we mean when we refer to Him as our "Father in Heaven." Just as your parents created you, He created the world (and everything in it, including your parents, etc.). And like a parent loves a child, so does God love you, only infinitely more. His love is truly unconditional — without bounds, provisions, or limits.

In sum, God has the perfect profile for your prayers. There is nothing He does not want to give you and there is nothing He cannot give you. What else could you want?

So, it should be clear that prayer is neither a reminder nor a wake-up call to the Supreme Being. What then is it all about?

It is all about **YOU!**

That's right…you. Prayer is actually not for God at all; it is for you. Unlike ancient rituals in which people brought sacrifices (sometimes of the human variety) to appease or please the gods, your prayers are not needed by God. In fact, being perfect means that God has no needs at all (see Chapter One, p. 22 for a more detailed discussion of this concept).

Prayer, logic insists, can only be an exercise for your own benefit. It is a process of introspection. It helps you clarify and refine who you really are, who you should be, and how to achieve the transformation.

Prayer, therefore, is actually a sophisticated vehicle for self-knowledge and self-improvement. And to the extent that we improve ourselves through prayer, we become more capable of absorbing and incorporating God's blessing.

Rabbi Nosson Scherman, in the Overview to the Artscroll Prayer Book, said it best:

> People always question the need for prayer — does
> not God know our requirements without being
> reminded? Of course He does, He knows them better

than we do. If prayer were intended only to inform God of our desires and deficiencies, it would be unnecessary. Its true purpose is to raise the level of the supplicants by helping them develop true perceptions of life so that they can become worthy of His blessing.

...Thus, prayer is the soul's yearning to define what truly matters and to ignore the trivialities that often masquerade as essential.

▶ The Secret

Were about to detail the Five Steps that can bring you the "advantage" you want in getting your prayers answered. But before we do that, permit me to mention the primary concept, or "secret formula," that really headlines the successful prayer experience.

The concept is nearly 3,000 years old, pre-dating the First Temple Era, and its author is none other than our own King David.

King David said, "The Almighty is near to all those who call unto Him, to all those who call unto Him in truth" (Psalms 145:18).

Truth means sincerity. Truth means being real. Prayer is the key to forming a relationship with God. And the cornerstone of every positive relationship is truth. Honesty. Being real. Trust, belief, and full confidence. That's why King David revealed this secret to us. Without our truthful expressions, intentions, and emotions in our prayers, God is "turned off."

"When you are ready for a real relationship," He says, "be sure to get back to Me. Until then you're only fooling yourself."

I'll prove it!

So convinced am I that "truth" is the master key to unlocking the gates of prayer, that I am prepared to prove it to you.

I'll prove it with a story. (Yes, a true story, of course.) I call it, "The Atheist's Prayer." You'll soon see why.

> *Many people who visit my school, Aish HaTorah, The Fire of Torah, in the Old City of Jerusalem, are tourists who come to Israel to get a sense of Jewish culture and history.*
>
> *One day a young visitor walked into my office. I started to ask him some questions about himself, and soon we were having a nice conversation. After about 10 minutes of pleasantries and "Jewish Geography," he interrupts me and asks, "Rabbi, do you believe in God?"*
>
> *(Some question!)*
>
> *"Sure," I say.*
>
> *"Rabbi, do you really believe that God speaks to man? Do you believe in miracles? Do you believe in revelation? Do you believe that stuff?"*
>
> *So I say, "Listen, Jeff, take a look at me. I'm a rabbi. It's obvious I believe these things. Why would you ask a rabbi such a question?"*
>
> *He says, "Well, because I've been speaking to you for 10 minutes and you seem to me like an intelligent man."*

(Now he's thrown me a gauntlet. He's telling me in so many words that intelligent people don't believe in this sort of nonsense. This is commonly known as "Chutzpah!" But our friend is laboring under a major misconception. This poor guy assumes that the Jewish people haven't really thought about how we know that these things are true. He is about to learn a thing or two.)

> *So I say to him, "You've got to tell me who brought you into my office today."*
>
> *He says, "Why do you want to know?"*
>
> *"Because I want to give the guy who brought you here a medal. Anybody who can get an atheist like you to come to speak to a rabbi —*

especially an atheist who also doubts that rabbis
have any intelligence — deserves a medal,
wouldn't you say?"

"No," he says, "the guy who brought me here
doesn't really deserve anything."

(And he goes on to tell his story.)

It seems that Jeff was visiting Norway and somehow found an opportunity to come to Israel. He decided it's now or never and he came. Of course, once a Jew gets here he's got to come to Jerusalem. And once he's in Jerusalem he has to see the Old City and the Western Wall, the last vestige of the Temple Mount during the Second Temple Era, nearly 2,000 years ago. It is the holiest Jewish site in the world.

When he gets to the Wall, he is amazed. Like so many others, he "feels" something. He is unprepared. He thought he would see some old stones...an archeological site. But he felt something that he could only describe as "heavy." He had some sort of spiritual experience.

He tells me, "You know, Rabbi, it's true. I am an atheist, but somehow a prayer came out of me that day. And it went like this:

> *"'God I don't believe in You, I don't know that*
> *You exist. But I do feel "something," so*
> *maybe...just maybe...I'm making a mistake.*
> *It is a possibility. And if I am making a mistake,*
> *I want You to know that I'm not fighting You,*
> *I have no quarrel, and I have no reason to*
> *be against You. It's just that I don't know that*
> *You exist.'*
>
> *"'God,' the prayer continues, 'I still think I'm just*
> *talking to a wall, but "just in case" You are really*
> *there, and I am making this mistake, then do me a*
> *favor and get me an introduction.'"*

Jeff finishes this prayer of his and slowly, in reverence, backs away from the Wall. Just then, he feels a hand on his shoulder. He is so startled that he jumps up in the air. He turns around and snaps at the fellow who touched him, "What's the idea of putting your hands on me. What kind of nerve ..."

> *The fellow is very apologetic, "I saw you praying and I just wanted to ask you if you wanted to visit a yeshivah."*
>
> *"What's a yeshivah?" asks our hero.*
>
> *So the fellow blurts out, "A yeshivah is where you learn about God."*

Jeff looks at me and continues his story:

> *"When this guy said that, it was as if he hit me right between the eyes! I had just finished asking God for an introduction and here is a guy pulling me by the shoulder and saying, 'Come on, I'll introduce you to God.' So — of course I'm gonna come. But that guy really deserves no medal for bringing me here. He didn't do a thing. Maybe God brought me here. But I want you to know, Rabbi, that you darn well better prove that He exists."*

Jeff ended up enrolling at Aish HaTorah for six weeks. He turned out to be a very serious student, and went back to the U.S. with a commitment to continue learning and to lead a Jewish lifestyle.

A year later, Jeff came back to Israel and told me the end of his story.

> *He said that one day, during that previous summer, when he was studying here in the Old City, he saw a very pretty, sweet, religious girl walking by. (He could tell she was religious because even though it was summer, she was dressed very modestly.)*
>
> *He said to himself, "Look at the charm this Jewish girl has. May the Almighty help me meet a nice Jewish girl like this."*
>
> *He didn't say a word to her. Weeks later he went back to Harvard. One Shabbat morning he walked*

> *into a synagogue and actually ran into the same*
> *girl he had seen in Jerusalem.*
>
> *He had to say something, of course. "It can't*
> *be," he said, "but you look like somebody I saw*
> *last summer in Jerusalem, in the Old City."*
>
> *She replied, "Yes, I was there...and I saw*
> *you too."*

You guessed it. They are now married and living in New Jersey.

Jeff was an atheist, but he got his prayer answered on the spot. Why? There can be only one explanation.

"The Almighty is near to all those who call unto Him, to all those who call unto Him in truth."

The power of sincerity is so overwhelming that even an atheist can get God's attention. Jeff called out to God in a genuine search for truth. His request was a real attempt to engage God in a relationship. Such a prayer, yes, even from an atheist, cannot be ignored.

So, "truth" is the central theme that permeates each of the Five Steps that can help get your prayers answered. The first three steps revolve around your relationship with God. They are solid litmus tests so that you can check whether you are in reality vis-à-vis your relationship with God. The last two steps focus on whether or not you are in reality with yourself! Do you really want what you are asking for and is it really good for you?

Let's spell out the Five Steps in detail.

Step One: Anticipate the Good

Capacity and desire — these are the two defining characteristics of God's relationship to His creations. And what a combination it is! Imagine. He has the full capacity to grant you any request — the perfect job, a fabulous relationship, talents galore, brainpower, health, a soft autumn breeze, great wine, contact lenses, ANYTHING YOU WANT! And, on top of that, He wants nothing more than to give it all to you...as long as it's good for you. INCREDIBLE!

If living in complete reality with God is truly your goal (and it should be), then simply imagine God as your parent — your "Father in Heaven," perhaps.

Got it?

Good.

Now, imagine calling your father one day and requesting a meeting with him.

> Dad: Sure thing. What do you want to meet about?
>
> You: Oh…it's no big deal…I'll tell you when we get together.
>
> Dad: Okay. See you later.

Later…

> Dad: Okay, son, what's the big secrecy about?
>
> You: I told you, Dad. It's no big deal…it's just…er…just…umm…
>
> Dad: What? What it is already? It's probably about money, right?
>
> You: Well…I guess I need a loan.
>
> Dad: Money problems again? I thought you were over that already.
>
> You: I don't need it for long…and I…uh…don't need too much either.
>
> Dad: All right. All right. How much do you need?
>
> You: I think a nickel should be enough.

When Dad hears how much money you want (5 cents), what is his most likely response?

- *Yes?*

- *No?*

- *I'll think about it?"*

- *Wait a couple of weeks?*

- *Let me see your latest credit report?*

NONSENSE!!!

His most likely reaction is, "ARE YOU FOR REAL?? THIS IS AN INSULT!"

Nobody would grovel to his father for a nickel, as if he is half-expecting not to get it. It is an insult of the highest degree! And when you do, you are demonstrating that you and your father have absolutely no relationship to speak of! A stranger would sooner give you a nickel in a flash!

Think about it. God's got a lot of nickels. How many? An infinite amount of them. After all, He MADE them. As a matter of fact, to the Creator of all — including your gastrointestinal tract, the Himalayas, DNA, etc. — EVERYTHING IS REALLY A NICKEL! God exerts no greater effort when He creates the Mediterranean Sea than when He imparts to us the know-how of manufacturing a spoon. And, by the way, when your Dad, or anyone else, gives you a nickel, he is a nickel poorer. Not God. God cannot be diminished.

Think about it. Even a billion dollars is "nickels" to Him.

In fact, if you stop for just a second you would realize that whatever it is you are asking for is infinitesimally less than what He has given you already!

Here then is the upshot of it all. Humility is fine. But when we plead and grovel and beg for things in a way that implies we are not certain we'll get them, we lose touch with the reality of Who God really is and what the relationship is really about.

When we anticipate that our prayers will be answered, we are praying and living with the reality that God can and wants to grant our every request. That is real prayer!!

What's our problem?

The question could be posed, "If God knows all, is able to fulfill all our needs, and wants only our best, why are we left with so many problems?" In His omnipotent way, God can help us avoid any problem even before it takes place. Why isn't He taking better care of us? Wouldn't any parent do that?

There are many loving parents out there who would like nothing more than to help their children avoid difficulties in life. And if you are one of them, or if you have one of them, or if you know one of them, you probably know that there is one thing that parents can never do for their children — they cannot live their lives! No matter how loving, powerful, or well-intentioned they may be, parents cannot control the lives of their children. The frustration is sometimes enormous and the pain can be overwhelming, but if you really love your kids, you allow and encourage their independence.

Being independent is what makes a human being meaningful. No good parent would deprive his child of the joy and the accomplishment of making meaningful choices. Without them (and the inevitable mistakes that tag along), our kids would just be robots. Their lives might turn out to be very nice, neat and correct, but they would also be bereft of meaning and true satisfaction.

God is no different. If He wanted to create us as angels or robots, He would have. But He didn't.

What He did do is create each of us with the potential for greatness. He instilled within His children the power to choose (see Chapter Six on Free Will) and to make decisions that are eternally meaningful. In order for that to happen, those choices must be made independent of God's intervention and will. That is why, with all His power, God still won't live our lives for us. He gave us the space we need. And it is a gift of infinite proportion.

So, if you don't really expect good things to happen, God is not going to invade your space. He "wants" you to relate to Him as you would to a real "Father in Heaven," but He wants you to work for that understanding.

Red light — green light

Let me give you an example of how this dynamic actually works.

Imagine you have a 25-year-old son, David. David has his first important business meeting in Washington Heights, the northern section of Manhattan. He needs to drive from Battery Park, the southern tip of Manhattan, during rush hour in mid-July. The traffic is bumper to bumper and if he doesn't get there fast the deal will vanish.

David could use some help...from anywhere he can get it. Red lights...gridlock...honking...summer heat...in other words, a-g-g-r-a-v-a-t-i-o-n.

Now, if you could somehow, miraculously, be able to control the traffic conditions for David, you certainly would. Zing...ding...green light...green light...E-Z Pass...whatever. You'd get him there on time, if you could.

Truthfully, David does have a father who can arrange this trip for him. It is his Father in Heaven, of course. After creating the Everglades, uranium, and the Milky Way, a little N.Y.C. traffic congestion should be relatively simple for Him, don't you think?

When David remembers this, he begins to relate to the Almighty in a very real way. He expects the traffic to begin flowing, and so it does. God is more likely to clear the congestion for David because David (remembering the charge from King David), calls unto God in truth — anticipating that God can and wants to give him a swift, safe, and smooth ride uptown. Of course, things are not quite as simple as that; other factors can also affect God's response. But relating to God in this real way — by anticipating the good — is a most advantageous factor in getting the response you desire.

Meanwhile, back on the streets of New York, David, eschewing the highway traffic, is breezing up 10th Avenue, rarely even touching the brake! Green light! Green light! He's "tuned in" and flying high.

But then David has a sudden reversal. Amazed at the ease in which he is traveling, he responds the way most of us would.

Man, this is just too good to be true!

And what is God's response to this flight from reality?
RED LIGHT!!!

Explanation:

By labeling God's natural demonstration of His power and will as being "too good to be true," David has now altered the relationship. God has "no choice" but to turn the lights red in the hopes of jarring David back into reality — the reality that ridding 10th Avenue of a few cars and red lights is just "nickels" for Him. It's not "too good to be true" at all! The red light is the mechanism for re-focusing that God employs to "remind" us that we must always be cognizant of His role in our lives as a true "Father in Heaven."

If David is focused enough to understand the true meaning of the red lights, he will adjust his own internal compass and re-direct his understanding of the clear road ahead as being totally consistent with something any loving father would do — if only he could. Once his focus is back in place, the green lights may then indeed resume.

When David reaches his destination, the REAL problem begins — finding a parking space on Broadway. Following our model, if you (David's loving parent) could now arrange for a stretch limo to pull out of a legal spot at the very instant that David arrives, you surely would. Again, God can easily arrange that. "Nickels," you know.

And so, the limo does actually begin to pull out just as David arrives.

> *"I can't believe my luck," he says! "This is really too good to be true!"*

What does the limo do? Pulls right back in.

Again, the first step in being real with God is to remember that you are talking to your father. A father who not only wants to help you, but can help you — effortlessly, no less. Anticipate the help. He's on your side. He'll answer your prayer. Bank on it!

Step Two: Be Shocked

The second aspect of being real with God is to be utterly shocked if things don't go the way you expected them to. It is the natural corollary to Step One. When your request is denied, it is as if you asked your father for a nickel and he actually said, "No." Of course, you'd be shocked. "How could he not give me a nickel? There must be some explanation for this!"

Being real with God means expecting that if what you are asking for is good for you, it make sense for you to get it. And when you don't, logic demands that you be completely taken aback by the denial. If you are anything less than dazed, your perspective on God is off the mark.

For example...

Imagine you've just earned an M.B.A. from an Ivy League school. You also happen to be the son of the C.E.O. of a major finance corporation. Your future is pretty set. You're the envy of all your friends and colleagues. The likely scenario is for you to start at the firm at entry level with preferential bonus opportunities, work your way up the corporate ladder, and eventually take over when Daddy retires.

The hiring process begins with the required interview process and so you are scheduled to meet with personnel at 9 a.m., the first Monday morning after graduation. The meeting will surely be pro forma, the red tape that is par for the course. The hiring decision is moot, but you agree to play along.

> *Good morning. I'm Philip Schacter, you know, Ed Schacter's son. I'm here to see Mrs. Hilfer. We have a 9 o'clock appointment.*

The secretary responds with a blank look on her face.

"I'm looking here at the calendar," she says, "and I see that your appointment with Mrs. Hilfer has been canceled. I've been instructed to tell you that we are not hiring at this time. There are no employment opportunities for you at this firm for the foreseeable future. Kindly leave the premises."

Needless to say, you are stunned…traumatized! How could your father have betrayed you like that?

God is the C.E.O. of this world. You are His son. Obviously, you are in line to receive every conceivable advantage. Merely being disappointed when your request is rejected is a reaction that is totally inadequate. Unless you are shocked, you are not living in reality. You must be bewildered…and, more importantly, you must ask, "WHY?"

Step Three: Listen to the Message

Uncle Max was close to all his nieces and nephews, but he was especially fond of his oldest nephew, Mark. That's why Uncle Max was rather perplexed by Mark's lack of response to a variety of correspondence that Max had sent. In the three months that Mark had been away at college, Max wrote two letters to Mark, three e-mails, and had left several phone messages.

Max wasn't worried. There was no urgency to the letters he sent. He merely inquired about Mark's welfare, adjustment to college out of state, and his course load. But he was a tad annoyed. "Is a brief note asking too much," he wondered?

But then he came upon a plan. Max was a clever fellow and he implemented the following strategy. He decided to write to Mark one last time.

> *My Dear Nephew Mark,*
>
> *How are you? I hope that college is treating you well and that you have, by now, adjusted to your new schedule and surroundings. Beginnings can be difficult, but you've always coped well in a variety of situations.*
>
> *I'd love to hear about the courses you are taking and the people you have met. Please drop me a line when you can.*
>
> *All the best,*
>
> *Your loving Uncle Max*
>
> *P.S. I've enclosed a check for $500 for you to use as you please.*

And then Max proceeded to seal the envelope and deliberately omit the check.

You guessed it. It took less than a week for Max to receive the following letter from Mark.

> *Dear Uncle Max,*
>
> *So nice of you to write. College is great and I am coping admirably with all the changes. Enclosed*

please find a listing of the courses I am taking
along with a small blurb, describing each one.

Please send my best to Aunt Sally and the rest of
the family.

Love,

Mark

P.S. You seem to have forgotten to enclose the
$500 check in your last letter. Thanks!

The third step in helping to get your prayers answered is to pay very close attention to the answer you are getting — especially if the answer is "No." This is not so easy to do. Most of us tend to sulk when we are rejected. We feel depressed, forlorn, angry, or resentful. We wonder:

Why couldn't I have gotten that great job?

How come I missed the lottery by just one number?

Doesn't God want me to get married?

These are all important questions. The problem is that we usually ask them rhetorically. We don't really want to understand the answers, we just want to complain or feel sorry for ourselves.

Mastering Step Three means being very serious about understanding the meaning of the denial of your request, while remaining fully cognizant that even a "No" response is somehow good for you. Being completely real in your relationship with God requires you to remember that an All-Powerful, All-Loving God is always teaching you. And a teacher can only be effective when He has your full attention and confidence. The "Teacher Supreme" finds a multitude of methods to get your attention — it may come in the form of a reprimand from a supervisor, a rejection from a spouse, a health-related issue, or maybe just traffic on a lazy afternoon. Like Uncle Max, God will do whatever is necessary to try to get you to focus on what you need to learn or change. But ultimately it is you who must attune yourself and interpret the message being conveyed.

Of course, interpreting the messages you receive is a difficult task. Figuring out exactly what is the appropriate lesson you should be learning, takes loads of practice, great motivation, and some assistance from Above, too. In fact, praying for the Divine Inspiration needed to help you understand your personal messages is a good way to demonstrate how great your motivation really is.

Remember, God is not arbitrary or unfair. He doesn't punish you unless you deserve it and can also learn something from the experience. All He wants is to educate you to help you become greater. If you become bitter, that's a sign you have forgotten Who God is and how much He truly loves you.

One more story — this one true.

> *A young man once entered my office at Aish HaTorah several years ago and announced proudly, "You don't need to teach me about God, Rabbi, because me and Him are very, very close. In fact, God does miracles for me!"*
>
> *"Really," I said. "Perhaps you could offer me an example or two of these miracles you say you were involved in."*
>
> *"Sure, Rabbi. Once I was riding my bicycle, here in Israel, up a winding mountain road. Suddenly, out of nowhere, a truck swerved into my lane, coming straight at me! I knew immediately that if I didn't get out of his way, we'd crash. I had no choice. I turned my wheel hard, and off the side of the road I went. Turns out, I found myself falling over a cliff, fifty feet down, on very rocky terrain. I screamed, 'GOD – HELP!'*
>
> *"In seconds, I hit the ground, and guess what...not a scratch! NOTHING! I fell fifty feet and God somehow cushioned me between the stones. A true, bona fide miracle!"*
>
> *"Amazing," I said. "A miracle, indeed. I have only one question to ask you, though. Tell me my friend — **WHO DO YOU THINK PUSHED YOU OFF THE CLIFF IN THE FIRST PLACE?"***

The point is quite clear. God is not Superman. He doesn't wait until you fall off a cliff and then fly in at the last second to save you. He is always there. He controls everything in your life — the problems and the solutions. He sent the car, He forced this fellow off the cliff, and then He saved him. Why? Only one reason. He wanted to get his attention. He wanted to teach him something. What? That is for him to find out.

Of course, falling off cliffs is a rather dangerous learning methodology. You'd be far safer and better off asking God now:

- *What do I need to learn?*

- *How should I change?*

- *What will help me reach my potential?*

And while you're praying, you might as well throw in a little request that should He find the need to get your attention in the future, perhaps fifty-foot cliff drops could be re-formulated into something a bit less perilous. That would be nice.

Step Four:
Focus — What Do *You* Really Want?

NOTE: The first three steps helped you focus on your relationship with God. These final two steps shift to your relationship with yourself. Together, these five steps give you a working paradigm for how to best approach God in complete truth, the truth that tells you what you really want out of life and what God's role can be in that process.

Question: If you were a billionaire, and you had a 7-year-old son, and one day he asked you for $10 million, would you give it to him?

Answer: I SURE HOPE NOT!

The reason no sane billionaire would give his little son $10 million is not because he cannot afford it. The reason is because that much money would clearly be harmful to a small child. (By the way, it's not especially healthy for anyone else either!)

Now, you also want $10 million; so do most people. But if you don't know why you want it, or if you should want it for the wrong reasons, then there is really no difference between the 7-year-boy and you.

Reminder: We don't need to use our prayers to "remind" God about what we need. It's silly. Prayer is really about choice. What we choose to pray for makes all the difference in the world.

Step Four in our model requires that you be specific in understanding exactly what it is you are asking for and why you want it. Simply put, if you don't know why you want something, you won't be able to use it properly when you get it.

Demanding of yourself that you clearly understand why you want something brings you to a higher level of maturity and responsibility.

> • *It forces you to clarify what it is you really
>   want out of life.*

And:

> • *It guarantees that you focus only on things that
>   are really good for you.*

This last point is essential. Like the billionaire father who would never give $10 million to his 7-year-old son, God is never going to give you something that is really bad for you, as long as your intentions are really good. There are plenty of things that come your way that may seem negative or harmful, but these are only placed on your table as growth opportunities. Every time you eschew a potentially damaging stimulus or experience, you grow in character and spirituality.

When you live in truth with yourself, you become an expert at judging what is really good for you and what isn't. Deep down, most of us are very much in touch with reality. When we toss away the distractions, the temptations, and the static, we are quite adept at discerning the difference between the positive and the negative.

Permit me to relate a story — this one is personal. It goes back to when I was 8 years old.

The World's Fair

I grew up on the Lower East Side of Manhattan and attended a local religious school about nine blocks from my home.

I recall that when I was about 8 years old, a thrilling event occurred — the World's Fair came to New York City. Nothing could be more grand: the exhibits, the rides, the fanfare — everything you could possibly want from a spectacle of utter delight.

One day my entire class decided to play hooky from school and go to the World's Fair. The notion tickled my little bones immensely. However, there was one condition. Everyone had to bring along a dollar of his own. The class leaders declared that "freeloaders" were not welcome. If you didn't have a dollar, you just couldn't come along. Period.

Now, when I was that age, there was only one way I could get a dollar out of my father — I had to earn it. And "earning it" meant memorizing an entire chapter of Mishnah — the Oral Law. There was no way in the world that I had enough time to memorize a whole chapter, so I resigned myself to the reality that everyone would probably go without me.

But instead of staying home that day, I realized that I could, at least, be a hero by being the only one to show up to class! Too much learning with no one there was unlikely, so why not earn some "Brownie points" for coming to school?

Morning arrived and I began my sad trek to school.

Suddenly, it hit me!

> *Wait a minute! What if I found a dollar on the street? People do find money in the street some-times. I could find a dollar and still go on to the World's Fair!!*

Hope...at least I had hope. I had found coins on the sidewalk before; maybe I'll get lucky today.

I started looking down. One block...two blocks...no dollar.

I began praying. Surely, God could send me a dollar if He wanted to.

Please God, you've got so many dollar bills up
there; all I'm asking for is one of them!

Two more blocks...no dollar in sight.

"Maybe God wants something from me," I thought.
I started promising. "I'll take out the garbage every
night...I won't fight with my sister..."

Another block — no luck. No dollar. I decided to up the ante.

Please God. How about a loan? Give me the dollar
now...on account...and I'll learn the chapter by
heart in the future! You can trust me! Okay?

No luck. No dollar.

The journey continued. I was running out of time, feeling desperate. I came around the corner and saw the dreaded school building in front of me. This was it; the moment of truth had arrived! I pulled out all the stops.

"O Lord," I cried, "just give me this dollar bill now,
and I'll never, ever, ever do anything wrong for the
rest of my life!"

I stopped in my tracks and listened to the words I had just said.

"Noah," I said to myself, "who ya kiddin? If you find
the dollar, you're going to play hooky from school!!"

I didn't find that dollar. I had to go to school and settle for hero status. But I did find an important lesson. Prayer only works when it's real. God is not about to give me anything that I know myself is not good for me.

Before you pray ask yourself:

- *What am I asking for?*

- *Why do I want this?*

- *Is it really good for me?*

Focus.

Be real with yourself.

Know what you want and know why you want it.

Then get ready. You might just get it.

Step Five: The Effort

As the saying goes, "Prayer is great, but talk is cheap!"

Make no mistake about it. Prayer is a most essential tool in any worthwhile endeavor in life. It is not an escape from responsibility or a desperation pass into the end zone with no time left on the clock. It is a potent and vigorous instrument to help us be real. But prayer, without action, is an empty, hollow mechanism that is doomed to frustration and failure.

"God helps those who help themselves," they tell us. And they are right. When prayer becomes a crutch — the lone weapon in your arsenal of acquisition — it bears mighty testimony that your desire is sorely lacking. An 8-year-old boy in search of a dollar prays to God, but he still understands that he has to walk the streets and peer at the sidewalk if he hopes to have his prayer answered.

Think about it. Why should God bother to take your prayers seriously when you don't demonstrate the same level of sincerity? It takes a decent measure of gall to expect God to "move mountains" for you, while you "merrily row your boat gently down the stream."

Even our patriarch Jacob heeded this creed of action. When preparing for confrontation with the imposing armies of Esau, Jacob utilizes prayer as only one piece of his strategic armory. He sends numerous gifts to bribe Esau, devises sophisticated military tactics, and then prays to God.

The Torah is teaching us a fundamental point. You cannot pray for something you're not prepared to go to war to attain yourself. God cannot allow prayer to become a substitute for being responsible.

How about YOU?

But beyond the message that your concentrated effort sends to God, is the message you send to yourself. Having to go all out for what you want makes that desire real to you. It's not just a pipe dream. It forces you to confront your motivations seriously.

- *Do I really want this?*

- *Is it worth the price I am paying?*

- *How much am I willing to sacrifice for it?*

And action keeps you in check every step of the way.

- *Am I getting there?*

- *Do I still want this?*

- *Is it right for me?*

- *Are my goals realistic?*

Making a genuine effort compels you to be real with yourself and to be in constant touch with where your life is going.

Let's review...

The God to Whom we pray is All-Knowing, All-Powerful, and All-Loving. There is nothing He cannot do for you and nothing He doesn't want to do for you. Prayer is, therefore, not a wake-up call to God or a reminder for Him, so He can know what you need. Prayer is not for Him at all; it is for you. Prayer is a vehicle for your own growth and development.

The "secret formula" that really headlines the successful prayer experience is the realization that you need to relate to God and to yourself in a state of total reality. He is your Father in Heaven and you are His child. As long as your relationship remains true, the lines of communication are open. When you forget who you are and Who God is, God responds by giving you corrective messages.

Step 1: Anticipate the Good
The normative response is for God to grant your requests. Expecting the positives means you are living with the reality that God can and wants to give you everything.

Step 2: Be Shocked
If things don't go smoothly, be genuinely surprised. Why wouldn't my father want to give me a nickel? What does it mean?

Step 3: Listen to the Message

Try to understand the meaning of the response you receive. God is always guiding and teaching you, keeping you on course, if that is where you want to be.

Step 4: Focus on What You Want

Focus. Understand what it is you are asking for and why you want it. And remember — God will only grant your request if it will help you in some way.

Step 5: The Effort

God helps those who help themselves. Prayer is not a substitute for responsibility. Making a genuine effort also compels you to be real with yourself.

God is always waiting for your call.

Pick up the phone today.

3 **KNOWLEDGE**

Picture the following scene:

Y ou're walking one sunny day, somewhere in Northern Iraq. You meet an infidel. He is on his way to Iran, planning to murder some Iranian radicals. You stop him to ask a quick question. The question is rhetorical.

> *Isn't it true that if you were born just 200 kilometers to the east, in Iran proper, you might well be coming up with your gun to kill yourself right now?*

Chances are, he would have no answer for you. At this moment, he feels that he is on his way to do "the right thing." A justifiable act. A noble deed. A "mission of conscience," perhaps!

But suppose he were born in Serbia — he'd also be convinced that he was right, but he wouldn't be a Muslim, he'd be a Christian and marching on to Kosovo to kill the Muslims. If he were born in China, he'd likely be a communist. And if he were born in Haiti, instead of a gun he'd be waving voodoo pins. And shocking as it may seem, if the same person were born in the ultra-religious Jerusalem neighborhood of Meah Shearim, he would be peace-loving, content, and waving his *tzitzis* (fringes) instead of a weapon.

This scenario should frighten you.

It should compel you to ask one of the scariest questions you will ever ask:

How can we be sure of ANYTHING??

If all of our values, beliefs, and principles stem from the society in which we live, then maybe, just maybe, everything we believe in is only an outgrowth of an accident of birth!

In short, how do we know what we know? How do we know that what we perceive is actually reality?

A step further

Now that we've got you scared, we'll take it a step further. The following statement is a bold one, but quite true: Not only can we not be certain that what we believe is really so, but the vast majority of people on this planet are clearly living their lives in error!

Allow us to explain — it's just simple math.

Consider that there are over a billion Christians in the world, 1.3 billion Muslims, three-quarters of a billion Hindus and half a billion Buddhists (to name just the largest groups). Every one of them is saying that all the other religions are totally wrong. Everybody is sure that he is right and the "other guy" is way off. Each belief system dictates that the various religions must be mutually exclusive. So they can't all be right. Somebody is right and the rest of them are wrong. If the Christians are right, then nearly 4 billion people on earth are wrong. On the other hand, if the Muslims are right that there is no God but Allah, and Mohammad is his prophet, then 3.7 billion other people on earth are wrong. If the Buddhists are right and there is no God, then perhaps 5 billion people on earth are wrong. If the Jews are right, then loads of people are way off base. It really is simple mathematics.

And yet, so many of these people are passionately convinced that they are right...to the extent that some of them would even be willing to kill the others who they say are wrong, or be willing to die themselves for their beliefs. They are so sure they are right.

Again, how do we know what we know?

Meet Jeff Korman

Let's try to illustrate the dilemma in a more personal way.

Imagine that your name is Jeff Korman. You're a lawyer from El Paso, Texas. You're walking down the street in Jerusalem and you see a sign that says: "Jeff Korman - El Paso - Jerusalem - Attorney at Law."

"What a coincidence!" you say, "I've got to meet this guy." You knock on the door and someone answers.

> "Come on in," he says. "Who are you?"
>
> "I'm Jeff Korman," you tell him.
>
> "Jeff Korman," he replies. "Isn't that a coincidence?"
>
> "It sure is. And I'm a lawyer from El Paso too."
>
> "That's amazing. Where in El Paso?"
>
> "Well, I live on Clark Lane, number 10," you say.
>
> "10 Clark Lane! Wait just a cotton-picking second! That's where I used to live. What's your father's name?"
>
> "Jack."
>
> "What's your mother's name?"
>
> "Alice."

Now the Jerusalem Jeff Korman is getting pretty steamed.

> "Hey — that's my mother and father. You're an imposter. Or, if this is some kind of sick joke, I don't like it."

> *"But...but..." you stammer, "that is where I live and these are my parents."*

And then you see through him.

> *"Hey, you can't have the same parents and the same name as me. You're a fraud. I know I am Jeff Korman!"*
>
> *(How dare this man from Jerusalem accuse you of assuming his identity, when the reverse is true?)*

Of course, you know that there are extreme cases in abnormal psychology of people who assume identities of others. The more ambitious people say they are Napoleon or Queen Elizabeth. But somebody, perhaps less ambitious, might decide to become a nice lawyer from El Paso. This fellow is obviously mentally unstable.

But what does he do? Instead of admitting his canard, he turns the tables on you and says, "Man, you are nuts and I am calling the police to take you to the looney bin."

After a few minutes the police come. Relief, you hope, has finally arrived. But, strangely enough, after a cursory few minutes of questioning, you find that the police officers actually believe him! After all, he is known in Jerusalem. He has a thriving practice, along with many clients, all of whom know him as Jeff Korman, and they are willing to vouch for him. You are just a guy on vacation in a strange city with nobody on your side.

The situation is strange, hypothetical, but far from impossible.

The question is: How do you know that you are right? How do you know who you are? The situation requires that you must convince the police, because this man is insisting that you are assuming his identity and he wants to press charges.

But your confidence isn't shaken. You are Jeff Korman. You know that. Calmly, you'll just offer them your wallet. You'll show them your passport, your driver's license, and your credit cards — all good evidence of identity with your name, your picture, and your address. You reach into your pocket, but your wallet is missing! You lost it. Perhaps it was stolen. What dreadful timing!

The man from Jerusalem reaches into his pocket and he comes out with all sorts of identification. They all have your name, your vital statistics, but his picture! Now whom are the police going to believe?

And what about you? Are you still sure that you're right? Or is your confidence shaken a little? Could it be that you lost your mind and he really is Jeff Korman, not you? No, no. Some people with less of a grip on reality might begin to doubt themselves at this point, but you are still sure that you are who you are.

You are convinced that this guy went to a lot of trouble to get forged documents. But mentally ill people who assume the identities of others are quite capable of doing such things.

You hit upon another idea. Let's call up Mom. You'll call the operator and ask her to connect you with the police in El Paso, Texas. They will verify that Mrs. Alice Korman of 10 Clark Lane is on the line. Then the police in Jerusalem will be sure of whom they are speaking with and your mother will set them straight.

Okay, they get your mother on the phone and they explain the bizarre situation to her. Hopefully, she can identify the voice of her son. They put you on. "Thank God, Mom, you were home to help me."

But instead of solving your problem, she says, "Who is this? The connection is not so clear. Is this Jeff or the imposter?"

You are speechless. The Jerusalem Jeff then gets on the phone and, to your horror, she says, "Jeff, my baby, I told you not to go to the Middle East. There's so much trouble there. When are you coming home?"

How could your mother make such a mistake? Even with poor reception, your mother should have recognized your voice. Is the imposter so skilled — even at voice impersonation? You have no explanation for this. You have walked directly into an episode from the "Twilight Zone." Are you still sure you're right? Is your mother senile or is it you who are mentally off? How can you know?

The fact is that you have to have a firm grip on reality so that even under these circumstances — where your own mother is challenging your very identity — you know, unshakably, that you are right.

But you do and so you try one final line of attack. You start grilling the charlatan with questions:

- *Describe the house at 10 Clark Lane.*

- *How many rooms are there?*

- *Where's the kitchen?*

- *Is there a basement?*

- *How many steps down?*

- *Who lives on the right?*

- *Who lives on the left?*

- *Where's the nearest drugstore?*

- *Where's the post office?*

As your investigation progresses, the truth emerges. Mom verifies that his answers are way off base. The guy is a fraud. He may be able to fake you out to some extent, but there's no way he could know all of these details. Eventually his sham is exposed and you are vindicated.

There are times in life when our most reliable convictions may come under scrutiny. Doubt may suddenly be cast over beliefs heretofore considered sacred and beyond query.

Do not despair. You need to know that even in today's world of uncertainty — where people say there are no absolute truths, where "everyone is right, so no one is right" — you can still be sure about things.

The key is never to stop investigating. Even Jeff Korman, on the brink of losing his identity and his sanity, persevered. He prodded, he provoked, and, eventually, he prevailed. The truth materialized.

And so it is in life. Certainty can be attained as long as the search continues.

How do we know this?

We would all love to achieve this level of certainty that so often seems so elusive. How do we do it?

Let's begin by understanding that despite all the New Age philosophy to which you have been exposed, certitude is eminently attainable.

For example, take a look at your hand.

Now count your fingers.

Chances are there are five of them. There are those who defectively have four or six fingers, but the overwhelming majority of human beings have five fingers on each hand.

Now, how sure are you of this observation? Could you perhaps be convinced that you really have seven fingers or twenty fingers, or ninety? Unlikely. You know you have five fingers. This is what we call "five-finger clarity." No doubt about it.

Realize, of course, that there is a concept called "brainwashing." And we know that it works. There were American soldiers who were staunch patriots, who were willing to die for their country, but who, after being captured by the enemy in Korea and in Vietnam and subjected to several months of indoctrination, were vilifying the imperialists and capitalists who sent them to war. But even those soldiers, no matter what level of programming they were subjected to, could not be brainwashed into believing that they had seventy-five fingers. They might lose confidence in the policies of their country, but what they knew they knew. We do have confidence in some things.

We would like to have the same "five-finger clarity" about the vital components that make up our life philosophy. Our values. Our principles and beliefs. This is important because if we don't have clarity about our life, then lots of things can get very muddled.

Of course, we are susceptible to being influenced under pressure. But that is an indication that we don't have complete confidence in our beliefs. Truthfully, if you think your confidence level is as high as possible, you would have no compunction about walking in to your local Rev. Moon type retreat and joining for a month or so, "just to see what it's like." No fears, no doubts. You could stride right into the storm center of "Hurricane Brainwash" without any qualms or hesitation.

Ask yourself:

- *Would I be willing to expose myself to Rev. Moon, Branch Davidian, or Hare Krishna style indoctrination?*

- *Would my belief system withstand the pressures it would surely undergo?*

- *Could I send my children there without concern for their values?*

In order to gain that level of confidence, you need to get a solid grasp on how we know what we know.

▸ What about God?

In today's Western world, it has become popular to declare that there are no "absolute truths." Everything is in doubt. It's impossible to know anything for certain. Thousands of philosophy courses on campuses worldwide profess and disseminate this most fashionable dictum. And the reason for its popularity is rather obvious. It's comfortable. Very comfortable. The implications of this assertion are exactly what people are looking for today — comfort and abandonment of responsibility.

> *I can't really be expected to do anything about something that is so uncertain.*

And so, intellectualism replaces action. Philosophical debate actually poses for responsible behavior. It's a charade, a tragic one, as we continue to pretend that truth is too elusive to capture.

The most distressing example of this travesty is the notion that we cannot know if God really exists. The indoctrination of this pretense is rampant. But if you use your own perception, if you forget for a moment that your society conditioned you to believe that there are no absolutes, you would realize that either there is a God, or there isn't a God. He doesn't start existing if you believe in Him, and then fade out when the atheist denies Him.

Either He's there and the atheist is making a mistake, or He's not there and the believer is making a mistake. You can't have it both ways. The philosopher is unsure, but Judaism says we can know.

Having real knowledge means that in life there are many things that you really can know, including the knowledge of the existence of God. What could be more important than knowing if there really is a Divine Being who created every proton, neutron, and electron in the universe and still controls the events relevant to every organism in existence?

And how do you attain this knowledge? First, by accepting that you have an obligation to discover the truth. And second, by realizing that if you search diligently, sincerely, with the willingness to find the truth, you will find the truth. And if you don't have the truth it's because you have not yet searched thoroughly enough.

Just because you may not know exactly where the truth lies does not exempt you from the mission to find it. On the contrary, it further behooves you to undertake the task. World leaders, religious or otherwise, may not agree on what the truth actually is, but they clearly agree that the truth can be known.

Imagine...

Imagine you were to get a personal audience with the Pope, and you would ask him if it's really true that no one can get into heaven, no matter how good a life he leads, if he doesn't embrace the fundamental beliefs of Catholicism. Perhaps he would hem and haw a bit, but eventually he would probably admit that that is indeed the theology of Catholicism. And if you tried to argue that it might not be so fair, he would say, "Sure it's fair. If you are really searching for the truth, and are sincerely and honestly willing to change and pay the price, then long ago you would have found out that joining the Catholic Church is the only way to get to heaven."

You might disagree (and you should), but he clearly states that the truth is quite attainable.

Similarly, if you were to go see a respected Muslim cleric, the scenario would go about the same. The only difference might be that he would end up saying, "If you are really searching for the truth, and are sincerely and honestly willing to change and pay the price, then long ago you would have found out that there is no God but Allah, and Mohammad is his prophet." He, too, makes it clear that an absolute truth does exist.

And even if you were to go see Fidel Castro in Cuba, and you would ask him about your chances of going to heaven, he would probably tell you that only communism can create a worker's paradise. If you were a real truth-seeker, instead of just trying to amass your wealth on the backs of the poor, you would know where the truth is at. "The truth lies here," says Castro.

The scene shifts...

Now imagine that you also went to see a philosophy professor at a major university who is giving a lecture entitled "There are No Absolutes." You decide to challenge his views publicly and tell him, right in front of his class, that people like him are undermining morality in the world, and sooner or later, he will have to answer for it. You cap off your diatribe with, "And I am sure there's a special place in the worst part of hell that is reserved for the likes of you!"

The plan works; he grabs the bait. He doesn't like being called "immoral" and being accused of bringing down the standards of humanity when he sees himself as the paragon of virtue and liberating humanity! His veins are bulging at his temples and he is barely able to control his rage, as he snaps back, "Look, son, the first thing you need to know is that there is no such place as hell. But, if there were such a place, it's people like you who would be frying there. Because it's fanatics like you that are bringing all this discord into the world. Now, if you had the courage to open your antediluvian head just a tiny crack, to allow the light of reason to penetrate that murk, then you would see that what I'm telling you is true — there is no absolute truth."

In other words, in his view, the absolute truth is that there is no absolute truth!! CHECKMATE!

You see, all over the world, human beings basically agree on one thing: that you really can know the truth. We all agree that if you search diligently and sincerely, with a willingness to pay the price, you will find the truth — MY brand of truth.

The case has been made that there is truth out there. The real question is, "How can you be sure that you have it?"

The answer is: Once you have the tools to really know what you know, you will be able to judge for yourself if what you believe is the truth or not.

As we have already established, you are certain of the fact that you have five fingers on each hand. You don't have to hear all the different points of view before you can comfortably reach that conclusion.

The fact that somebody out there might claim that you have seven fingers, or twenty-one fingers, does not, in the slightest way, diminish your confidence level. You have so much empirical evidence to support your five-finger claim that it is an unshakable conviction.

Judaism has always said: We have to get the same five-finger clarity about our beliefs and values.

Like a chain

Our knowledge base can be compared to a chain. Even a heavy steel chain is only as strong as its weakest link. If the chain has just one link of tin in the middle, it's practically worthless. It is better to have a shorter chain; at least it's of some use.

The same holds true for our knowledge base. If we don't identify and isolate our areas of confusion — the tin links in our chain of confidence in our beliefs — then those areas can weaken the strength of the whole chain. But when we identify those areas of confusion, then we know what we're unclear about; and those areas of uncertainty can be isolated so they don't hold us back from maintaining strong convictions in other areas. Isolating the confusion separates the strong links in our knowledge base from those weaker links that need to be bolstered with more information and education.

The real key to knowing what you know is having the ability to place your conviction in the proper category. Too often, we assume — automatically — that all of our beliefs are "pretty much" of a similar ilk and level of certainty.

> *I guess if I believe in something, I really do*
> *believe it.*

Not exactly.

There is belief and there is belief.

There are actually four different categories of certainty. And knowing into which category your particular belief fits is the secret to recognizing real truths when you see them.

- *Knowledge*

- *Belief*

- *Faith*

- *Socialization*

Each category represents a totally different level of conviction that can best describe all of your beliefs and values.

Knowledge is something of which you are absolutely confident.

Belief is a conviction for which you have some evidence, but lack complete information.

Faith reflects a desire to believe something, even though there is no evidence to support it.

Socialization means accepting an assumption because society has conditioned you to do so.

Becoming an expert in properly filing where your convictions belong allows you to evaluate how much weight to assign to each particular opinion you have. For instance, you should never let a "faith" in anything important conflict with something you consider to be "knowledge."

Additionally, appropriate labeling of your beliefs helps you see which ones need some shoring up and which ones could be discarded. Once you realize that a value you have treasured forever is really not more than a "socialization," it should compel you to gather some real evidence for it, in order to fortify the notion. If, however, your search fails to garner enough information to transfer the notion to "belief" or "knowledge," you may consider tossing it away!

Fine-tuning...

Let's see if we can "fine-tune" these categories, so you'll know exactly how to use them most efficiently.

"Knowledge" is absolute confidence — you know you have five fingers; you know you didn't rob a bank this week.

But let's say I told you that your favorite cousin, Sammy, was just picked up for grand larceny.

"Impossible!" you say.

Really?

You cannot know that with "five-finger certainty." You do have historical evidence of your cousin's righteous character, but you can't be absolutely sure. Your confidence in your cousin's innocence may be termed "belief," but it is not "knowledge." After all, if someone appeared with witnesses and fingerprints and a video showing your cousin walking into the bank with a shotgun and saying, "Give me all your money," you'd say, "I never would have believed it."

"Faith" is a leap against logic; it is a product of desire. Have you ever gotten a tip on the market that supposedly guarantees you're going to triple your money in a month? It's so hard to turn down one of these tips because we all desire to make money quickly. A lot of people who otherwise have better sense still get fleeced because they love these tips. They have no evidence whatsoever that they will make money; they simply want to believe it. That is faith.

"Socialization" is a catchall term for all the ideas you accept as a member of any particular society. Your society influenced you — socialized you — to accept certain assumptions. Chances are that you didn't independently investigate what your society taught you. In America they say capitalism is right; in China, they say it's communism. In India, they say Krishna is god; in Italy they say it's Catholicism. Accepting these dictums usually has nothing at all to do with knowledge...you're just going along with the rest of the crowd. What a pity...

Not just theory

But being able to discern the certainty level of your convictions has ramifications that transcend philosophy, politics, religion, or Sammy's innocence. The implications are eminently practical.

You live in a real world, and you make judgments on your convictions all the time. It is important to know whether your convictions are based on knowledge, belief, faith, or socialization.

You decide to go into a partnership with someone. But first, you do your homework. You investigate. You get some information, like a credit rating, recommendations from his former partners, and references from his employers and employees. You find out all you can about him before you decide to trust him. You believe he is an honest man. It's belief, because it is based on evidence. Fine.

Or, you decide to get married one day. You want to believe that the person you are marrying is wonderful in every way. You better investigate good and hard. You better know what you can know. You can ill afford to make a mistake there. You better know whether it's blind faith or a rational belief based on some pretty good evidence — not just a feeling or intuition.

Of course, you can't know everything with five-finger certainty. Some things you have to just believe — and often it is the wisest thing to do. For example, if somebody tells you that if you put your hand into the fire you'll get burnt, or if you walk too close to the edge of the cliff you could lose your balance and fall down, you should have enough trust to believe him. Gathering too much evidence in certain cases could actually be fatal. Sometimes believing is the right thing to do. But often, believing is simply not enough — you have to know.

The Bible implores us to get knowledge, wherever possible. God wants each and every one of us to investigate and ask ourselves: "How do we know this is true?" God has the confidence that if we use our minds, ask plenty of questions, and sincerely seek out truthful answers, then His existence and all of His truths will be abundantly apparent.

"From there you will seek Hashem, your God, and you will find Him, if you search for Him with all your heart and all your soul" (Deuteronomy 4:29).

A comprehensive quest for truth, with heart and soul, will lead to the discovery of God.

"You shall know this day and take to your heart that Hashem, He is the God" (ibid. 4:39).

First have knowledge — then take to your heart.

Judaism says: "Beware of any system that discourages questioning." Anyone who stifles questioning is afraid it may unearth the dishonesty of his beliefs.

▸ Watch those reactions

People who get angry when you ask questions are often betraying the weakness of their convictions. They lack true confidence in their beliefs. They are relying on blind faith and don't want anyone to ask questions that might undermine their house of cards. But if you know — if your convictions are solid — challenges don't threaten you in the least bit.

A good illustration of this concept is found in any high caliber, traditional Talmudic academy, where the biggest honor always goes to the student who asks the best questions. In fact, stories are told of students asking such good questions that they were appointed teachers in the rabbi's stead! It is that kind of scrutiny that must become the hallmark of all your personal evaluations and beliefs.

This is not to say that people don't have any convictions. Unfortunately, though, what most people are convinced about is that they are unlikely to change — or worse, that they are incapable of change. This is the worst conviction possible. Deep down, you know that's not true. Change only seems impossible because of fear. But if you are afraid to be really challenged, pay close attention to that message. The fear tells you that you probably don't fully trust your convictions. And that means you are unsure about some of the most important things in life. Embrace the challenge. Welcome the inquiry. Bask in the explorations that come your way. You'll likely emerge more confident, better equipped, and more at peace than ever before.

Practice

First, decide if each of the following statements is true or false. Then circle the category that best fits the statement.

Remember the definitions:

- **Knowledge** is something of which you are absolutely confident.
- **Belief** is a conviction for which you have some evidence, but lack complete information.
- **Faith** reflects a desire to believe something, even though there is no evidence to support it.
- **Socialization** means accepting an assumption because society has conditioned you to do so.

1. The world is round.	T	F	K	B	F	S
2. Rich people are necessarily happier than poor people.	T	F	K	B	F	S
3. Going to college helps people understand what they want out of life.	T	F	K	B	F	S
4. It is likely that most people's beliefs and ideas come from their societies.	T	F	K	B	F	S
5. God exists.	T	F	K	B	F	S
6. Chocolate ice cream is better than vanilla.	T	F	K	B	F	S
7. Edinburgh is the capital of England.	T	F	K	B	F	S
8. Women are more intuitive than men.	T	F	K	B	F	S
9. My mother loves me.	T	F	K	B	F	S
10. Democracy is superior to communism.	T	F	K	B	F	S
11. People are basically good.	T	F	K	B	F	S
12. All children can learn.	T	F	K	B	F	S
13. Capital punishment is a deterrent to murder.	T	F	K	B	F	S
14. There is no life after death.	T	F	K	B	F	S

15. Scientists are objective.   T F   K B F S
16. The Republican Party understands the free market system better than the Democrats.   T F   K B F S
17. Many of my ideas and opinions come from my society.   T F   K B F S
18. Corporal punishment should be allowed in schools.   T F   K B F S
19. America is the best place in the world to live.   T F   K B F S
20. It is wrong to steal.   T F   K B F S
21. Taking home a package of computer paper from one's workplace is not stealing.   T F   K B F S
22. Stress affects the health of one's body.   T F   K B F S
23. Citizens have the right to bear arms.   T F   K B F S
24. Stealing is illegal.   T F   K B F S
25. If you don't know what you would be willing to die for, you don't know what to live for.   T F   K B F S
26. Evolution is a more reasonable explanation for the origin of the universe than the Biblical account.   T F   K B F S
27. If you are kind and patient with others, they are less likely to be rude to you.   T F   K B F S
28. Canada is the second largest country in the world.   T F   K B F S
29. Smoking causes lung cancer.   T F   K B F S
30. There are several qualitatively different classes of pleasure available in this world   T F   K B F S
31. An intellectual is one who makes decisions based on facts rather than emotions.   T F   K B F S
32. We need to have goals in learning to get the most out of our study time.   T F   K B F S
33. There is no such thing as free will.   T F   K B F S

Conclusion

Knowing that you have an obligation to find things out should be nearing five-finger clarity at this point.

There is a popular saying that goes, "Hey, you never know!" While the adage is rather innocent, it is also quite dangerous. It suggests that true knowledge and real certainty are rarely attainable. What we have seen here is that such is not the case.

When something makes sense, you should have the courage to check it out. Don't just reject or accept concepts out of hand. Investigate sincerely. For if you investigate, you will find truth.

Might as well begin now.

4 HAPPINESS

Face it.

You spend your ENTIRE LIFE in the pursuit of happiness. True or not?

Welcome to the club.

You're no different than billions of other people just like you, just trying to find the road to true happiness.

The search is literally endless.

Money. Power. Prestige. Material possessions. Love. Entertainment. Knowledge. Drugs. Relationships. Sushi. Cosmetics. Respect. More money. Alcohol. Fitness. The "perfect" job. Climate. Therapy. Smiling a lot. Exotic vacations. A spa. Music. Sports. Herbs. Even more money. And on and on and on and on...

It doesn't work, does it?

And yet, the search goes on. "It must be there somewhere," you say. And like the teenage explorers hiking through ancient ruins and caverns, you seek the elusive "hidden treasure," convinced that it is "out there."

When you stop to think about it (and we seldom do), you probably realize that the hunt is fruitless. Generation after generation has followed the very same pattern and come up empty-handed. "We'll be different," you proclaim.

But are we? Seek out those who claim to have "tried" any of the above-listed elixirs of life and examine their results. Are they truly happy? Surely not. As a matter of fact, find those who have amassed ALL of the above tantalizers of life. Are they happy or do they continue this endless pursuit — hoping, praying that the NEXT milestone will be IT!?

We live in a "new and improved" generation. No answer will suffice unless it is the product of a NEW technology, a NEW study, or a NEW methodology. Only if the formula is "CAN ONLY NOW BE REVEALED," do we lend it genuine credence.

But maybe it's time for a change. Maybe some of the answers can only be found by looking back — perhaps at an OLD book, with wisdom that is ancient, yet prudent and farsighted.

We speak of a collection of the early writings of Jewish antiquity, a book that was canonized as part of the Oral Law (Talmud) in the year 190 C.E., called "Ethics of the Fathers." It is a virtual instruction manual for moral and ethical behavior then and now.

In it, the Sages ask, "Who is rich?" (Things haven't changed much, I guess.)

Their answer bears analysis.

> *"The one who is happy with what he has" (Ethics of the Fathers 4:1).*

In other words, if you appreciate what you have, you'll feel rich. If you don't appreciate what you have, no matter how much you get you'll never be satisfied.

That's why a Jew starts every morning with a series of simple, yet poignant blessings. "Thank you, God, for giving me life. Thank God, I can see. Thank God, I can use my hands and feet. Thank God, I can stand up straight, etc." Judaism teaches that if you can master the art of noticing, appreciating, and consciously enjoying what you already have, then you'll always be happy.

You're disappointed. You were hoping for some elaborate, clever answer — a "secret" and complex formula that might require sophistication to understand yet be relatively simple to implement. Instead, what do you get? APPRECIATE LIFE!

> *"Big deal," you say. "Teach me something I don't*
> *know already."*

People often forget that teaching is not simply the art of imparting knowledge heretofore unknown; it is the art of conveying concepts in a way that enables people to utilize the information in a productive fashion.

Most of us may already know that appreciating life's pleasures is a valuable construct. But if so many of us know it already, why are so many of us so unbearably unhappy??

Apparently, something is wrong, somewhere.

▶ A gift of happiness

I once met a young man who possessed an unusually happy disposition. His countenance compelled me to find out more about him.

> *"What's your secret," I asked him? "How do you*
> *manage to be so happy all the time?"*
> *"I got a gift of happiness when I was 11 years*
> *old," he explained.*
> *"A gift of happiness? From whom?"*
> *"From God."*

It seems he was riding his bicycle one day when a gust of wind came and blew him off the bike — right into the path of an oncoming truck. The truck ran over him, tragically severing one of his legs.

As he lay there bleeding, the thought struck him that he might have to live the rest of his life without a leg. Naturally, a deep sadness enveloped him. He was very depressed. Incredibly, while still in the street, writhing in pain, he realized that being depressed isn't going to get his leg back. With or without his leg, he decided, right then and there, that he is not going to spend the rest of his life in total despair and self-pity.

He was brought to the hospital, and soon after, his parents arrived. They stood over him, grieving, as loving parents would, "What's going to be with him, the poor child...without a leg, this is terrible..."

> *But instead of joining in their refrain of tears and anguish, he turned to them and said, "You know, you're going to have to get used to this."*
>
> *They looked at him in amazement. "We've got to get used to this?? We are filled with pain and torment, knowing that you will have to adapt to a whole new way of life! But you've got to get used to it!"*
>
> *"Not really," the boy said, "I'm already used to it."*

"Ever since then," he explained to me, "I see my friends getting upset over trivial things: their bus came late, they got a bad grade on a test, somebody insulted them, whatever. But I just enjoy life."

What clarity did this young man attain at the startling age of 11? That it doesn't help to focus on what you don't have! It just drags you down. It wastes your energy and doesn't produce a thing. The key to happiness is to take pleasure in what you do have!

Clearly.

Let's focus...

Remember when you were 16, 17, or 18 and you thought that if only you had your own car, you'd never be miserable for the rest of your life? Or if only you met "the right girl," if only you had "a better job...," if only..."

And then, a "miracle" happens. You actually get the car! Result? For a whole week you're riding on a cloud and walking on air. You can't believe your good fortune. Life is beautiful. And then...the car overheats, you get a ticket, parking becomes a hassle, your best friend got a nicer car...you go right back to being unhappy again. You have fallen for the classic myth of Western society: "Happiness is dependent on what you own."

Judaism reminds us about reality: "Happiness is not a happening. Happiness is a state of mind. You can have everything in the world — and you can still be miserable. Or you can have relatively little and feel very, very rich."

The following example brings the point home in rather dramatic fashion.

Imagine...one day you are working in your office on the 70th floor of the Empire State Building. You get up from your chair and walk to the window for a quick moment of distraction and a refreshing view of New York City. To your utter shock, you are greeted by a man on the ledge, expressing full intent to leap to his death.

> "Stop!" you call out instinctively. "Don't do it!"
>
> "Try to stop me and I'll take you with me!" he counters.
>
> Noting that the guy is 6'5", you re-assess your options. "I feel like I'm either in a bad movie or on Candid Camera," you say to no one. "I guess I've got to try to talk the guy down, for whatever that is worth."

The dialogue begins:

> "I suppose I'm expected to try to talk you out of doing this," you fumble, as your opening gambit.

It falls kinda flat.

> "Do what you want," he says. "My mind is made up."
>
> "Well...I've never done this before, but I think I'm supposed to ask you why you are doing this."
>
> "I can tell you," he says, "but believe me, it's not gonna help. You still wanna hear?"
>
> "Sure."

"Well…to begin with, my wife of thirty-two years just left me. My kids are totally a mess…not working, not happy, and no longer talking to me. Then yesterday I lost $2 million, my life savings, on a sweetheart deal that went bad, if you know what I mean. The S.E.C. began a full inquiry into my company and I haven't got a single friend in the world. Wanna hear more?"

You don't. But your new friend continues anyway… for another 40 minutes, detailing every possible misery a human being can encounter in a lifetime. By the time he is finished, you're ready to jump with him.

His tales of despair have rendered you speechless.

"So, big shot," he challenges, *"can you give me one remotely sensible reason why I should go on living? Huh?"*

The pressure is on. You cannot deny that his gloom is entirely appropriate and yet, you also know that suicide is just not the answer. What can you say to him?

Suddenly, you get a flash of inspiration.

"Sir, I've heard your woeful tale and I know your life is as miserable as could be. But try the following experiment. There's nothing to lose; you plan on jumping any second anyway, right?"

"Okay, okay, I'll try your silly experiment. Just make it snappy."

"Close your eyes for a minute. I want you to imagine that in addition to all your misfortunes, you also suffer from another personal calamity. You are totally blind. No colors, no sights of children playing, no fields of flowers, no sunsets, no beauty, adventure, or stimulation of any kind is available to you. Got it?"

"Yeah…yeah…what's the point of…"

"Just bear with me. Now imagine that suddenly there's a miracle. You open your eyes and for the

first time in your life you can see! Your eyes are actually functioning. The sensation is absolutely beyond description! Everything you've ever heard about and dreamed about is suddenly right there, before your very eyes!

"So tell me, are you still going to jump now? Or do you think you just might stick around for a week or two to see some of the wonders of this world?"

Your friend is silent. The ideas are percolating...you can see it.

"I guess I would stick around for a little while," he mumbles.

"Really," you say. "What happened to all the troubles you just told me about? They haven't disappeared!"

"Ah...I guess they're not so bad...anymore, that is. After all, now I can see!"

"EXACTLY! If you really appreciate that you can see, with all the wonders that come along with sight, then all your other miseries are suddenly shoved into the background! Your new perspective changes everything! Why? Because now you are focused on what you have rather than on what you are missing. Even when pain is all around you, how you view life makes all the difference in the world.

"Here, let me help you off that ledge."

On the other hand, if you take all that you have for granted, then nothing in life will really make you happy.

The secret of happiness is to really appreciate what you have. But don't expect that to come naturally. It's a skill which must be learned and practiced.

Let's clear up some misconceptions people have about happiness, so that once you learn how to appreciate life, nothing will be in your way.

Misconception #1: Once I understand what to do, the rest is comparatively easy.

Wrong.

Understanding something and doing something about it are very different. It's very possible to fully understand how to be happy, and still not do a thing about it. That's because subconsciously, many of us would rather be comfortable and unhappy, than endure the temporary discomfort of changing our habits in order to achieve lasting results. Learning any new skill requires effort. You have to be willing to invest the pain and effort to achieve real happiness.

Misconception #2: If I become content and satisfied with what I have, I'll lose my motivation to achieve more.

Wrong.

Nothing could be further from the truth. The fact is, happy people are energized. There's never enough time in the day to do everything they want to do. They're always ready to go! They're ambitious! Go over to a happy fellow and say, "Hey, you want to go fishing? I got a boat." He'll say "Great! Let's go!" Go up to a guy who's depressed and say, "Want to go fishing?" He'll probably say, "Maybe tomorrow. And anyway, they said it might rain."

Misconception #3: Happiness is optional. If I want to be depressed, that's my own prerogative.

Wrong again.

"Choosing" to be depressed is the epitome of selfishness. Have you ever gone on an outing with a bunch of friends on a beautiful Sunday afternoon? Remember the guy who always found something to complain about?

- *Who forgot the forks?*

- *It's too hot for volleyball.*

- *I want to go home already.*

Nobody wants to be around him. He's a "downer." You feel like saying:

> *Come on, what's wrong with you! Enjoy yourself or get out of here!*

When do you have an obligation to be happy? When you're making someone else miserable.

We recognize that it is wrong to spoil everyone else's fun by being miserable. But this applies to our everyday lives even more so than at an outing. How about when we're at home? With our spouse or with our kids? What about when we walk into the office with a hangover on Monday morning? Is it right to make others suffer because we had a bad day? Being happy ourselves is a big part of being considerate to the people around us. We need to remember that the facial expression we display does not really belong to us. It is visible mainly to those we encounter and to whom we relate.

Let's get practical

Now that we understand the common misconceptions, we are ready to discuss the tools for achieving happiness. They come in three levels of difficulty: easy, intermediate, and advanced.

The simplest way to begin appreciating life is to find some things you're really grateful for, and count them every single morning for one month. For example: your eyes, your feet, your thumbs; your children, your car, your imagination. Consistency is essential. Establish a set time each day to feel the gratitude and pleasure of having them. And let the depth of each pleasure really sink in. Contemplate every minute aspect of the pleasure they give you and watch your appreciation grow.

Here is an illustration to show how this works:

> *All of us have an uncle or a cousin or an aunt who just loves to complain. The next time you visit your aunt and she wants to complain, you say, very respectfully, "Aunt Gerty, you know I came here to suffer with you today. But before we suffer, it's only fair that you also tell me about five pleasures you had today."*
>
> *Of course, she will say, "What you are talking about? I had no pleasures."*
>
> *Don't give up. "Auntie, did you have coffee for breakfast?"*
>
> *"Okay, I had a coffee."*

Don't let her get away with that. Force her to share the pleasure.

> *"Was it sweet? Warm? Did the aroma linger? Did it give you energy?" Re-live the pleasure with her. (She'll have to do it because this is her ticket to complaining.)*
>
> *"Okay, it was sweet and it was nice and it was ahh..."*
>
> *"Good. Tell me about four more, Auntie."*
>
> *"I didn't have any more."*

Don't be discouraged. This is all very new to her.

> *"Did you wash your face? Was it pleasant? Warm? Cleansing? Refreshing?"*

Re-live it with her. Then discuss another one. Make her go through five simple pleasures. (There are hundreds, by the way.) Then watch what happens. Her complaints won't disappear, but after she goes through five pleasures, her complaints won't sound nearly as bad.

If you really want to work at this, every evening when you come home from work, sit down with your spouse, sibling, roommate, or whomever and discuss one pleasure that each of you experienced that day. Just one! You'll be amazed how powerful this very simple exercise actually is. And don't forget about kids! Incorporating this little awareness into their daily routine slowly changes their perception of the world and of themselves! Anyone who is able to focus on the incredible gifts we all enjoy is on the way to genuine, bona fide, everlasting happiness.

The next exercise is more sophisticated. It requires a serious outlay of time — one hour, a small price to pay if it really works.

Have you ever gone to a doctor for a complete physical examination? Often, before the doctor sees you, you are asked to fill out a questionnaire about your past and current health history. Sometimes the questionnaire is quite comprehensive. You could be asked 100 – 500 questions about all the possible maladies and symptoms you might have experienced in your lifetime. Chances are that very few apply to you, but the enormous range of possible sicknesses that a human being can contract is absolutely staggering! Your ability to check the "no" column for so many diseases is a great way to appreciate all the intricate ways your body continues to serve you.

That said, try taking one hour to write down everything in the world for which you have to be grateful. This is not easy. You'll fly through the first 15 minutes. The next 15 minutes you'll slow down; don't worry about that. The next 15 minutes will get tough, but you can pull through if you include your eyebrows and your socks, etc. The last 15 minutes are totally excruciating.

Once the list is compiled, add one new blessing each day. The opportunities are infinite. Every day the depth of your appreciation will soar as you uncover new layers of heretofore unnoticed or under-appreciated blessings.

The power of this exercise is clear: In order to add new blessings, you have to be conscious of all the others. And that's when you really begin to appreciate how much you have.

Once you have accumulated a personalized and impressive list of the blessings in your life, you are ready for the final leap — prioritizing.

Ask yourself the following questions. Answer them and then create similar questions, tailoring them particularly for your own clarity of purpose and appreciation. These questions can be disturbing to some, but your answers will be revealing and insightful in the way they expose your truest interests and priorities in life.

If, for some reason, you were forced to choose either one pleasure or the other, which one would you select?

- Your eyes or your hands? Why?
- Your ears or your feet? Why?
- Your sense of taste or $5 million? Why?
- Meeting the President for 5 minutes or spending 2 hours with your kids? Why?
- Buying a foreign sports car or donating $50,000 to a hospital? Why?
- The most powerful PC available or understanding the formula for happiness? Why?
- An expensive wristwatch or a compliment from someone you respect? Why?

(Now compose seven more questions yourself.)

Notice how "weighing" the pleasures compels you to focus on how much pleasure each blessing provides and the different aspects of pleasure each one affords you. You need to think about why your hands are so valuable, what you would actually say to the President, and why compliments mean so much to you. This exercise forces you to focus on your life like you've never done before.

For those who want to become true connoisseurs of appreciation, prioritize your list. Over and over again. Follow this course and work at it constantly. Your gratitude will grow and grow, building a solid foundation to give you true happiness for a lifetime.

5 FREE WILL

"**H**ow precious is man, who was created in the image of God" (*Ethics of the Fathers* 3:18). You've probably heard this notion before — that man was created "in God's image," but what does that mean?

Well...for one thing, any being that is compared to God in any way has got to be incredibly powerful. But power can be understood in many different ways.

On the one hand, we have an intellect that enables us to perfect the world and gives us mastery over the universe. On the other hand, we have passions that can compel us to hurt each other and destroy the universe.

There is nothing like man who can harness the forces of this world for good. And there is nothing like man who can harness them for evil.

Man is more dangerous than the most vicious of animals. But

there is no creature alive that can match man's creativity or sense of beauty or kindness.

How are we to understand this dichotomy that, in many respects, defines humanity?

King David wrote a beautiful psalm while pondering this very question. Perhaps he can shed some light on this matter:

When I look to the heavens
and I see the work of Your hand,
the moon and the stars
which You have created,
I ask, "What is man
that You remember Him?
And what is the son of Adam
that You should care for him?"
You have made him
a little less than Divine,
And You have crowned him
with honor and dignity
(Psalms 8:4-6).

King David looked to the sky 3,000 years ago and was awed by God's creation. He compared himself to the infinite dimension of space, the mammoth expanse of it, and wondered: "What is man that You should remember him...that You should care for him?"

Did you ever stand under the stars in the countryside, where the glare of the city lights doesn't invade our space...a moonless night...no clouds...just an enormous expanse of stars in the galaxy? It is then that we can reflect on the reality that there are, in fact, billions of stars out there...millions of light years away from us. It is truly an awesome sight. And yet, in spite of man's seemingly puny size in relation to the rest of creation, King David recognized that "You have made him a little less than Divine." Just a "little less" than God! Talk about status... power...awe.

But what really makes us just a notch less than God Himself?

The answer is free will. Free will is the defining characteristic that allows mankind to resemble the Divine. It is the most central characteristic testifying that we were created in the image of God.

To be created in the image of God means that unlike all other creatures, we have been given a distinctive gift, a Divine spark within us that contains a facsimile of the Creator. That spark gives us the power to create or to destroy. It is that unique feature which gives us the awesome power to make choices.

▶ An even greater gift

Exclusive a gift as free will is, however, the Sages say that God bestowed upon mankind a gift that is even greater than free will. And that is the fact that the Almighty told us about this gift. Why is knowing about this an even greater gift? How do you put that into perspective?

To answer this question, imagine a group of homeless people who have taken up residence on a cold, noisy, and grimy street. Each has his own dilapidated shopping cart, spilling over with the most meager belongings imaginable. They beg for money; they sift through garbage pails for a piece of bread. It's a miserable existence.

Now suppose, in a flight of benevolence, you decide to give a million dollars to one of them. Imagine what he would do with all that money! He would buy a warm home, a comfortable bed, new clothes, a kitchen-full of groceries, etc.

There's only one problem. You hide the money in the bottom of his bag and he doesn't know a thing about it. He's schlepping around a million dollars, but he lives with the same misery, the same hopelessness, because he doesn't know what he has. What a tragedy.

The Sages are teaching us that while it's great to be created in the image of God, if we don't know what we have then we're basically living the life of a mule.

The gift of free will gives each of us enormous power and potential. But if we don't realize we have this power, then we can't take advantage of it. It is of no use whatsoever. We will have lived the life of a beggar, so to speak, when in actuality each of us is royalty.

As potentially powerful as free will is, it is greatly under-utilized and usually misunderstood. We frequently neglect to use it. In order to learn how to employ the power of free will to its fullest capacity, we need to clarify exactly what it is.

What exactly is free will? Is it the simple ability to exercise preferences — like when to sleep and what to eat? If that is free will, what makes us so different from animals, who also make these same kinds of choices every day? Perhaps free will is something more profound, like having the ability to choose between good and evil.

That is what most people think. Most of us believe that having free will gives us the capacity to choose between good and evil, something beyond the faculty of the animal kingdom. Certainly that is true...in part. But Judaism says that free will is much more than that.

The fact is that everyone believes that he is truly good. Every human being has an inherent desire to be good. He wants to use his potential, do the right thing, accomplish, and have meaning. No one wakes up in the morning thinking to himself, "What tremendous evil can I choose to do today?" Even the most wicked people in the world, underneath it all, want to be good...that's why they must rationalize their behavior and paint it as good.

For example, put Adolf Hitler, the emblem of iniquity and evil, in the same room with Mother Teresa. Ask them, "Which one of you is a good person?" Who do you think is likely to answer, "Me," more quickly? Hitler, of course! He'll revile and vilify the Jewish people for bringing depravity into the world, and seek your patronage in joining his selfless campaign to rid the universe of this vermin. Mother Teresa would probably blush about her meager attempts to stop world hunger and humbly apologize for not doing more good for the planet!

No. Free will is something much more than choosing between good and evil. It is, in reality, the most essential tool for everything we do in life. It is the choice between life and death.

How do we know this? Between that's what God taught us in the Bible.

"Life and death I have put before you...choose life"
(Deuteronomy 30:19).

And it is shocking how often we choose death. Let's explain.

What does the Torah mean when it says that free will is the choice between life and death? Don't we all want to live? Is there anyone who would not choose life? Isn't survival man's strongest instinct?

There are, of course, those who do not choose life. And in order to understand this better, let's analyze the ultimate "death" decision — suicide. What is a person choosing when he chooses to die? What is his motivation?

More often than not, his motivation is escape. He wants to avoid pain.

In the words of Shakespeare:

> *To be or not to be, that is the question. Whether 'tis*
> *nobler in the mind to suffer the slings and arrows of*
> *outrageous fortune, or to take arms against a sea of*
> *troubles and by opposing end them? To die, to sleep,*
> *to sleep, perchance to dream...*

That's what Hamlet and any person who contemplates suicide is looking for. He wants to sleep. He wants to avoid being awake. The pain is just overwhelming.

Truthfully, there is always a pull to run away from unbearable pain. Many of us feel like quitting at any given time of the day. Free will is the constant choice between confronting the challenge, in other words living, or running away, which really means dying.

This life and death/free will choice process is constantly at play in our lives. In a sense, we are all deciding at this very moment whether to take the necessary pain in order to grow in life or to quit for the day and "put it off for tomorrow." This "death decision" can be of the extreme variety — suicide, drugs, alcohol, etc. — or it can be much more subtle, that is, by killing time.

Most of us are expert time killers and, while occasional time killing is entirely acceptable, perhaps necessary, many of us have perfected it to a bloody art form. Today, "leisure" has replaced growth. Channel surfing, web surfing, exotic vacations, "just vegging out," gorging, checking your e-mail every 5 minutes, bar hopping — you name it; the escape list is endless. We often vacillate between being "totally bored" and "completely stressed out." And either way, our response is the nearest escape route. Killing time is suicide on the installment plan. You could use that time productively, but it's easier to check out. It is the quintessential free-will choice — to live or to run away from life, and in effect, die.

Deep down, we all want to be great; we all want to change the world. It's just that we don't always feel like putting in the effort. So, we distract ourselves and escape from who we really are and what we want to achieve. And when we escape problems, we escape being great — as great as we can be.

Every moment we're alive, we're using our free will to choose between life and death, reality or escapism. Whether we are aware of it or not, we are in constant conflict between those two choices. And how we resolve that conflict is where our greatness lies. Our greatness is found in using our free will to live, fight, and accomplish — rather than run away.

In order to win the battle and master the awesome power of free will, we need to understand the five stages to this conflict. As with anything, the strategies for winning, the how-to's, are relatively simple, but making them part of your life takes a lot of practice. Somebody can tell you how to play basketball in 15 seconds — aim at the rim, hold the ball, throw. No big deal. But it will take an awful lot of practice before you get that ball in.

It is the same with life's great lessons. Telling you about free will takes just a few minutes, but to make the most of this great potential takes a lot of practice and a lot of effort. But it's worth every moment of the investment.

Right this very second you are making a decision — whether to continue reading or to stop. You may be thinking, "Do I really want to know about free will? This is too heavy. I'd rather be watching TV right now." Or you may be thinking, "This is interesting and important; I must read this carefully." Whether you continue reading or stop and put the book down, you will be making a decision. But are you consciously aware of making that decision? Probably not.

Stage One

Life is a constant stream of choices. The first stage of mastering the power of free will is to become aware that you are making choices all the time. Once you become sensitive to this fact, you can then begin to monitor and examine your decisions.

Have you ever had the experience where you got into your car, turned on the engine, and then just ended up at your destination without remembering any of the turns you made along the way? You have absolutely no recollection of having made a 20- to 30-minute trip. Yet, you must have made hundreds of decisions during that time: when to speed up, when to slow down, what to look at, when to turn. Some of these decisions were probably critically important. Imagine all this, and the entire experience is a complete blank in your mind!

Even if the trip you just made was not especially important and the decisions were rather inconsequential, life certainly matters. Don't make your life one big blank! Become aware! You decide!

One of the common criticisms of some organized religions is that they can breed a system of ritual that encourages doing things by rote, without thought and consideration, and therefore without meaning. How many of us, in our own lives, go about our daily chores and routines by rote? How many actions did each of us take today without conscious thought? (Thousands, for sure.)

If you really want to gain an appreciation for this concept, keep a journal in which, at the end of each day, you record five significant events of the day. You will see that your days will become bigger, and your weeks more significant. At the end of the month, you will be a bigger person, because you will have more "you" to accompany you.

Complacency is the enemy of free will. Someone who is indifferent about life and the events around him is one who is casting his or her free will to the wind.

Don't be a zombie, acting and reacting without thinking about what you are doing and why. Do not allow yourself to be simply swept along on some tide of action or feeling over which you have no control. Don't let your decisions just happen. Take control. Ask yourself, "Is this the decision that I want to be making?" And if it isn't, then don't do it!

Your decisions are what shape your life. Living with that awareness means you are using your free will actively and not passively. By getting on top of your decisions, you are taking charge of your destiny.

Stage Two

Second stage of free will is: Don't be someone else's puppet. Be your own person. It's not enough to be aware of your decisions; you need to be certain that they are your own. You must take responsibility for them. Live your own life. To achieve greatness, every person needs to evaluate the basic assumptions and guidelines he or she uses to make decisions about life.

This does not mean, however, that your every thought, conclusion, and philosophy must be self-generated, quite the contrary. Utilizing the teachings and instructions of our sages, leaders, and role models is a vital part of our process of formulating our own decisions in life. But we need to make them our own.

Don't automatically accept society's assumptions as being valid unless you've thought them through and agree with them. In everything you do, live for yourself — not for society, or for your parents, or for your friends.

And just as you should not be someone else's puppet, don't become a prisoner of the decisions you made five, ten or twenty years ago. Start each day anew. Reevaluate where you are in life in order to be sure that what you chose then is what you would still choose now. In other words, make sure it's you guiding your decisions, not your decisions guiding you.

Just because you decided on a particular career five years ago doesn't mean it is still the best thing for you today. Your current well-defined value system may have been in total consonance with the "you" of a decade or two ago, but does it still withstand the test of time? Is it still working, considering what you now understand about life and its priorities? Don't assume that because you decided at one time there is no compassionate and involved God on earth, you can't find more evidence today and make a more informed decision. Check your assumptions and goals to make sure that they are really yours. That's the key to being your own person and using your free will effectively.

Stage Three

Thus far we have said that the effective use of free will requires, first, a keen awareness of the constant stream of choices that we are making and, second, the capacity to be independent. The greater the proportion of our actions that arise out of a conscious choice and the greater the degree to which we are prepared to think independently and to take responsibility for our actions, the more effective we will be as human beings.

The third stage of mastering this most treasured power is recognizing that in the human condition there is a fundamental life and death struggle with which we are constantly faced — the struggle between the body and the soul.

Your body usually chooses death — meaning, the yearning to live a pain-free existence. The body seeks transitory comfort and sensual pleasures. The body wants to drown in passions, to procrastinate, and to quit.

But the soul is fighting the body every step of the way. Your soul is the true image of yourself, representing the person you truly want to be. Your soul is your drive to reach your potential and to attain something beyond yourself, which is greatness. Your soul strives for meaning and clarity and purpose and to attain all things ultimately good. Your soul wants to grow, tackle challenges, and overcome obstacles. It wants to "live," in the fullest sense of the word. Stage three is huge. It means really coming to terms with this battle of body vs. soul.

Jogging is a great example of this classic struggle. Sooner or later, just about everybody confronts the great "Jogging Idea." In the collective health/fitness conscience of Western civilization, jogging is seen as something we all "should" be doing. But inevitably, the internal battle begins.

- *Can't wait to go out there for the early morning jog.*
  It sure is cold outside…

- *Pretty soon I'll feel better and look better!*
  Sure…if the strain doesn't kill me first.

- *I'll probably live longer too!*
  What's so great about old age?

This is illustrative of the classic kind of body/soul conflict.

And the same kind of battle really takes place in thousands of areas of our lives:

- *It's important to understand free will. Pay attention.*
  Who needs this? I've been doing just fine until now. Besides, it sounds like a lot of work.

- *Let me take an inventory of today's accomplishments and mistakes so I can better plan my day for tomorrow.*
  Great idea, but I'm too tired. I'll start tomorrow night.

- *It's wrong to take those pens home from the office.*
  Aw…my boss expects to lose some pens. He won't mind.

In order to win the war within yourself, to rule your own mind and thoughts, you first have to learn to distinguish between the cravings of the body and the aspirations of the soul.

Using your free will requires that you be aware of the opposing options presented by your body and your soul. Only when you bring these conflicts to the surface can you make a clear-cut decision and choose life. Until you can identify which voice inside you is speaking, your body or your soul, you cannot know which side of the conflict has your ear, and you cannot make an informed decision.

And if we don't understand what is going on inside of us, we can't know who is running our life — and chances are the body will take over. The body is a master manipulator and it is selling you the here-and-now, in living techno-color, with the commercial message being: AVOID PAIN AT ALL COSTS.

▸ Not like any other battle

A short but wonderful story is told which illustrates this very problem. A group of soldiers is returning home after winning a war; they are marching and singing, flushed with victory. A wise man meets them on the road and tells them:

> *Friends, you think you have achieved a major*
> *victory, but the truth is you merely won a very*
> *minor battle. It is only now that you will confront*
> *a major war — the war within yourselves (Path*
> *of the Just; Introduction).*

The task — the internal clash — is daunting, for three reasons:

1. When you fight a human enemy and win, you have peace, at least temporarily, until he regroups. In this internal war, even when you've just won the battle, there is no let-up. The enemy is after you again, immediately.
2. When you fight a human enemy and are defeated, you can often flee. Your opponent may chase you for a day or two, but if you run far enough, he will get tired and stop coming after you. In the internal war, no matter how far you run, the enemy will keep coming after you.
3. When you fight a human enemy and he breaches your camp, you know you're in real trouble. You do everything in your power to prevent that from happening. In the internal battle, the enemy has no need to breach the camp; he is inside your camp because he is you.

In summary:

What does the body want?   vs.   What does the soul want?

Comfort	Understanding
Sleep	Meaning
Indulgence	Productivity
Excuses	Accomplishment
Escape	Greatness
To Quit	Reality

When you're not aware of these conflicts you get ambushed. It is only when you bring these conflicts to the surface that you can make a clear-cut decision and choose life. Until then, you are in the dark.

Stage Four

Up to this point, we have come to recognize that there is an internal dynamic at work in all of us, which we identify as the body-soul conflict. In this context, we stated that the key to self-mastery lies in how the conflict is resolved. The next logical step is to provide a methodology. Our solution is called "Identifying With the Soul."

Identifying with the soul means taking the steps necessary to ensure that your free-will decisions are directed by your soul, not your body. Your soul knows what is best for you; it seeks wisdom, understanding, and clarity. It is the soul that drives you to be the best you possibly can be. The body needs to be attended to and even made to feel satisfied, but it shouldn't rule you with its misplaced desire and base motivations. If you allow your body to be in control, you can easily find yourself on a road to self-destruction. In other words, the fourth stage of harnessing the power of free will is: "Take care of your body, but live with your soul." Identifying with the soul means ensuring that the soul always has the upper hand.

The question is: How do you keep the body under wraps? What steps can you take to keep yourself soul-focused?

Think of the human being as a conglomeration of a soul, a body, and a mind. The soul is the real you; it is the taskmaster.

The body is the servant; it fulfills the soul's tasks. The mind is like a computer relay station — it services whoever is pushing the buttons. The key is making sure that the soul is always in charge.

How? By distancing yourself mentally from what your body wants and empowering your speech patterns to reflect the reality of your needs.

For instance, do not think, "I am thirsty." Rather, think, "My body needs some water."

Do not think, "I am tired." Instead, think, "My body needs sleep."

Make statements — verbally and mentally — that clearly differentiate yourself from your body. Your body is not you...it is only a part of you.

Imagine that you start feeling hungry. Don't automatically give in. NO HARM WILL COME TO YOU! Say to yourself, "My body claims that it's hungry and that if I don't feed it it's going to starve to death. Is that true? When was the last time I ate? It wasn't that long ago, was it?"

Another frequent scenario:

What happens, for example, when you are trying to diet and someone offers you a mouth-watering piece of chocolate cream pie? Your first reaction is, "No. I shouldn't. I'm on a strict diet." But your body tries to persuade you otherwise. "Just take a little piece, it won't hurt you." Or, "This is the absolutely last piece of cake you'll have, and tomorrow you'll begin the diet."

In order for you to get control of your body, you have to be clever. You have to use the very same tactics your body uses when it tries to convince you to do something you don't really want to do.

Do you appreciate the body's strategy? The body doesn't say, "Forget the stupid diet. It's okay to be fat. Have the pie." The body knows you'll reject that reasoning outright. So it lets you believe that you can just give in a tiny bit, while still being in control. But the body knows that once you go along a little bit, it will be harder for you to resist the next time. He's got you just where he wants you.

To be effective at winning the war with your body, you must employ a good counter-strategy. Beat the body at its own game.

Coax it the same way it coaxes you. Do you want to keep to an exercise routine? Don't tell your body, "From now on, every morning, fifty pushups." Tell it, "Just for the next 5 minutes, we'll exercise. And then we'll go have chocolate cake." Do you want to use your mind to study something worthwhile instead of just killing time? Tell your body, "Come on, let's just study for half an hour. Then we'll go watch TV." And the body will follow.

With this approach, your body will follow along. In reality, the body can "learn" to actually enjoy what the soul wants. But the soul can never learn to enjoy what the body wants.

These kinds of exercises help you to realize that the soul is the real you, not the body. And if you can identify with the desires of the soul, it will satisfy the needs of the real you. Your task is to train the body and coax it to reflect the reality of the soul.

Learning to identify with your soul molds your body to become a reflection of your soul. It results in an increase in the level of your free will, and thus to a development of self. That is stage four of mastering free will.

> *"The righteous talk to their bodily desires, while*
> *evil people let their desires talk to them"*
> *(Midrash Rabbah; Genesis 10:10).*

Who is running your show?

Stage Five

As a soul-based being, you are now utilizing your free will to near maximum capacity. Quite an accomplishment! But as a God-believer, you've got one final push that can send your power into the highest gear possible – stage five.

Stage five means you are one with the Almighty. You are where the real power lies. Stage five means that you've realized the aspirations of your soul and you are identifying with God.

Your main task in making this concept work for you is to be in the mode of constantly asking, "What does God want in this world? What does He want from me? That is all I want to do."

When that is your only motivational force, you will have achieved the highest form of living. When God's will becomes the sole focus of your attention, you will be using your power of choice to merge with the most meaningful and powerful force in the universe: the transcendental.

The conflict between the body and the soul is really a conflict between life and death. The body wants to die and the soul wants to live. The ultimate form of living is immortality — life without any semblance of death. Therefore, attaching yourself to God is attaching to the highest and purest form of life itself — nothing less than eternity.

That is the ultimate use of our free will. That's what the Almighty really means when He says in the Torah, "Choose life."

Make your will His will. If you do, you'll be what King David said you can be — just a little less than God Himself. You'll be His partner in changing the world.

Of course, there are many people walking around this planet claiming to be fulfilling God's will, when, in fact, their behavior totally belies that very contention. Be careful. The key ingredients in discovering God's true will are study and your choice of role models. There is no substitution for study in understanding God and His messages to us. Torah, Written and Oral, is God's communication to Man and therefore it is the most direct means of discerning His will.

And it follows that those whom we choose to emulate and learn from, need to be steeped in understanding and living His message. Without appropriate role models, we are swimming upstream with a very weak paddle.

Therefore...

Free will represents the ultimate potential in human beings. Most of us are walking around not really using our full potential. Humanity can perfect the world. We know we can make it a beautiful, loving place.

So, fight for clarity and master the power of free will. That is the road to greatness.

These are the five steps to mastering the awesome power potential of free will:

Stage One: Don't be a sleepwalker. Be aware of the decisions you are making at every moment. Make decisions actively rather than passively.

Stage Two: Don't be a puppet of someone else's assumptions and values. Scrutinize your own rusty and time-battered principles and ideals, as well.

Stage Three: Be aware of the conflict between the cravings of your body and aspirations of your soul.

Stage Four: Identify with your soul, not your body.

Stage Five: Make your will God's will.

6 | INTELLECTUALISM

Susan is driving along the Taconic State Parkway on a bright, sunny Tuesday morning when she thinks she hears a funny noise emanating from the engine. The car "feels" fine so she continues on her trip. Being the "careful" sort of girl she is, though, she takes the car into the mechanic later that day.

> *"I don't know too much about cars," she begins, "but my Mitsubishi was making a funny kind of noise today on the Taconic. Do you think you could check it out?"*
>
> *"Don't need to," comes the voice from under an old Hyundai.*
>
> *"Oh...I see..."*

Susan waits for the explanation that is sure to follow. It doesn't come.

"...er...and...er...why is that?" she inquires ever so gently.

"Because the problem is your air-flow sensor, that's why."

"Oh...I see...and...er...how do you know that without even checking the car?"

"No reason. I just have a 'gut feeling' that that is the problem. That's how I do all my work. The job will cost you $525.00...cash. Shall I start now?"

What should Susan do?

What would you do?

What would anyone do?

Is there really any question? Would anyone fork over $525 to a mechanic based on his "feelings"? I pray not. He's got to at least open the hood and pretend that his diagnosis is based on something!

And yet, Susan and millions of others (maybe even you) do exactly that every single day!

Not only that, but usually the decisions we make in this manner are far more crucial and significant than a few hundred dollars. And still we falter.

Decisions...decisions...

Name some of the really important decision-categories in life:

• Health (medicine)
• Love (marriage)
• Religion
• Finances
• Employment
• Major Purchases (house, car, appliances)
• Politics

Now see if any of these statements sound familiar. Have you or someone you know ever made a decision using this kind of reasoning?

• Health – "Why did I choose this doctor? Oh, I don't know...I met him and he really sounded nice and gentle."

- Love – "I always felt wonderful when I was with him."
- Religion – "When the guru (Rabbi, preacher, etc.) spoke, I just always felt inspired."
- Finances – "I just had a 'feeling' that stock was ready to go through the roof!"
- Employment – "It seemed like a nice place to work."
- Major Purchases – "I took one look at that car (house, cell phone, video camera, freezer), and I knew I just had to buy it!"
- Politics – "I'm telling you, she just really sounded sincere."

Sounds familiar? Of course it does. It happens all the time. But if we stop for a moment and think about it, we all realize that using this particular brand of "calculation" does not make a whole lot of sense. Feelings can often mislead you. The gentle doctor also happens to be inexperienced; love is blind; the charismatic guru turns out to be another Jim Jones or David Koresh; stocks respond to hundreds of market variables; and how often do you buy something on impulse only to find the same item someplace else for 25 percent less two days later? Not to mention the countless charlatans who are voted into office by overwhelming majorities! And yet, people frequently choose to live by what their emotions tell them rather than by what their mind tells them. Somehow, thinking something through is a process we often disdain.

As Bertrand Russell once noted, "Many people will sooner die than think; in fact, they do so."

We are swayed by our emotions. And decisions, even really important ones, somehow become objects of our whim, our fancy, and our sentiment. This is the reason that con men are so successful.

A true story that confirms how easily people can be manipulated is told by Larry Williams in a book entitled, "The Definitive Guide to Futures Trading." A trader sent letters to 10,000 clients. He advised 5,000 clients to buy a particular stock and the other 5,000 to sell the same stock. Naturally half of them made money. To the 5,000 who profited from his advice, he sent another two sets of letters, again telling half to buy and half to sell. Continuing his scheme, he once again sent letters only to the group who profited, splitting the group in half in the same fashion he had done before.

At the end of this process, he had a group of 1,250 clients who had witnessed him making three correct predictions in a row! To these, he offered a subscription to his special "investors newsletter" at the cost of $500, a small price to pay for "a sure thing." A simple, but brilliant scam. Just one example among thousands that happen all the time.

▸ What is an "intellectual"?

Making decisions based on logic, reason, facts, comparison research, referral, and sound advice from experts can spare you a lot of grief. That's using your head. Bottom line is, if you use your intellect to primarily direct your life, rather than your feelings, you have a much better chance of accomplishing your goals. When you do that, you are what is called a true "intellectual."

A person who thinks straight, without being confused by feelings, is an intellectual. He leads with his head, not with his heart.

Now simply being "intelligent" does not make someone an "intellectual." A person could be absolutely brilliant yet still allow his emotions to rule his life. The person who uses understanding to arrive at reality is the true intellectual, even if he doesn't have the highest IQ. The intellectual possesses the willingness and the foresight to take a step back, and then take the time and make the space to review the facts, before reacting or reaching a decision.

Of course, in the popular vernacular, an "intellectual" is often defined as a person steeped exclusively in ideas, someone who is lost in a world of thought and philosophical rhetoric. He is depicted as the antithesis of the practical person. The intellectual that we are characterizing, however, is quite the opposite. The true intellectual, as we are defining this term, is a profoundly practical person. Because he or she thinks things through in a sensible and cogent fashion, he or she is the person most likely to act. And because he or she thinks before acting, the action is likely to be reasonable, practical, and highly effective.

> *"What about my feelings?" you are shouting,*
> *no doubt.*
> *"Are you proposing that feelings don't count*
> *at all?"*

Your reaction is quite common and reasonable. Don't misunderstand. Our emotions are extremely essential. It is precisely our emotional responses to the situations confronting us that trigger our flow of activity. Human beings are certainly not robots. We must never be out of touch with our feelings. However, after that trigger has been set in motion, it then becomes vital to clearly distinguish between our emotions and our intellectual assessment of the situation, in order to make appropriate decisions.

When we allow our emotions alone, un-tempered by rational investigation, to guide our actions, we are likely to be fixated on the result that we want to see and not on the reality of the current situation. That is a very dangerous state in which to be.

Becoming an intellectual

Of course, it's not nearly enough just to know that your mind is your most indispensable mechanism in life. You've got to know how to use it to its maximum power! The mere knowledge that you are holding a Stradivarius is of no practical use unless you become a virtuoso violinist as well. The fact is that most computer wallop — speed, memory, and functionality — is usually wasted by the 95 percent of people who have it at their disposable, but have no idea what to do with it! What a shame it is that our minds never seem to work at even close to their full capacity.

This chapter, therefore, is about how to make the most of the power of your mind. You can get a black belt in karate, judo, jujitsu, kendo…in any or all of the many martial arts disciplines. And the techniques learned in attaining that belt can be utilized to flip over practically any man of nearly any size, no matter how much bigger and stronger than you he may be. But, if a rhinoceros charges at you, you abandon your techniques in an instant and you run to climb the nearest tree. No one tries to flip a rhino.

And yet, even though it is such an intimidating beast, the rhino is on the verge of extinction. Why? Because man has a mind. And with that mind, he invented a gun. Against the strength of man's mind, the mighty rhino doesn't stand a chance.

Just like you can get a black belt in the martial arts, you can also get a black belt in the intellectual arts. You can learn the steps of how to become a virtuoso of the mind and thereby school yourself into becoming a bona fide, masterful, and high-powered intellectual.

Of course, nobody starts out as a black belt. There are several rungs on the ladder of intellectualism that must first be climbed and mastered in order to reach the top. The white belt, orange belt, red belt and brown belt must all be attained before you are ready to complete your assent to the intellectual zenith — a true-blue, fully functioning black belt intellectual.

Unlike the different stages of pleasure described in Chapter One that can each be realized independently, the journey to the peak level of intellectual command must be made incrementally, building its potency gradually, acquiring one belt at a time. Only when you commit yourself to practice the skills necessary for each belt color and become a real expert in the utilization of those skills, can you hope to enter the elite class of the "Black Belt Intellectuals."

As we have discussed, an intellectual is a clear thinker. He does not allow himself to be misled by emotions. And the "white belt intellectual" knows that in order to think as clearly as possible, he must understand exactly what he and others are talking about. In order to do that, he must have definitions.

Example:

Question: Are you a "good" person?
(Most people are likely to answer, "Yes.")

Question: Tell me, are you a "bafoostig"?
(Most people are likely to answer, "Huh?")

Question: Just tell me, are you a "bafoostig" or not?

Obviously, this is not a question that anyone can answer, unless he happens to have a definition for "bafoostig." Without knowing what a "bafoostig" is, no one can say whether he is one or not. And yet, most people have no problem saying they are "good" even though they'd be hard pressed to define what a "good" person actually is!

Why is that?

Probably because without thinking the matter through with any clarity, we think of ourselves as being good by defining "good" in the negative sense. It's like we are saying to ourselves, "I guess I must be a good person because I'm certainly not a 'bad' person." But we all should realize that just the absence of doing bad things does not automatically make us "good" people. And even doing "good" things is extremely subjective.

Suppose you say, "I feel I am a good person." And a person who happens not to be your greatest fan disagrees. "I feel that you are not," he says. Who is to say who is right? What makes one person's feelings more valid than someone else's? We have to have a clear, objective definition of what "good" really is before we can know if we are good or not. Without a definition, we can't begin to evaluate whether we are or aren't something. All we can do is use our feelings, a totally subjective proposition.

Throughout time, scores of people have sacrificed their lives for causes they "felt" were good, when in reality, the objectives they died for were of little or no consequence, or actually evil. How many terrorists and insurgents have died while considering themselves "freedom fighters" for a just and noble cause? In reality, many of them die as wicked men, having wasted their lives without having ever accomplished their goal of being good.

The first prerequisite in learning to use your mind is to define your terms. Always get a definition. Break out of your subjectivity and get a completely objective understanding of the concept you are describing. If you use only your feelings to assess reality, you'll never get a clear picture.

Getting sound definitions on life issues, both major and minor, helps you focus on your goals, reach your aspirations, and measure your success.

- *What is a good person?*

- *What is love?*

- *What is friendship?*

- *What is the difference between someone who is stubborn, and someone who is intolerant?*

How many people are in a serious relationship and believe they are in love, only to find out later that infatuation had blinded them? If you want to be sure you are in love, and not infatuated, if you want to be sure that you are making the right decision in having a deeply significant relationship with this person, you need more than feelings. You need a clear understanding of what love is and what infatuation is; otherwise, you may be setting yourself up for a fruitless and painful experience.

You get the idea.

Once you have good definitions, they become the cornerstones of a rational way of life.

Let's play the "I–You–He" game

- *How do we know that feelings affect our objectivity?*

- *Isn't it possible to maintain our impartiality and detach ourselves from our emotional investment?*

- *How do definitions "save" us from the trappings of partiality and personal bias?*

To better understand these issues let's introduce the **I-YOU-HE** game. The rules are simple, the objective is rather obvious, and the ramifications are painfully transparent.

Scenario:

Steve and his partner, Dan, have a meeting scheduled for 12 noon. Budgeting his time poorly as he usually does, Steve leaves his home at 11:45 a.m. and picks up Dan for the normal 30-minute drive. In his quest to make up for lost time, Steve floors the accelerator and flies down the side streets, averaging about 85 miles per hour. When they pull in for the meeting, the dashboard clock reads "12:00." Whew.

The best way to describe Steve's driving is:

- *brave*

- *foolhardy*

- *reckless*

Answer: It depends.

It depends on who is doing the describing to whom.

Steve is proud that he accomplished the near impossible. He says to himself, "That was a 'brave' piece of driving. It took real guts to pull that off!"

Dan, holding on for dear life in the passenger seat, is likely to tell Steve, "Slow down, buddy. You're being 'foolhardy'!"

When Dan gets out of the car, out of Steve's earshot, he might tell anyone else who will listen, "That partner of mine is a 'reckless' idiot!"

When we are talking about ourselves, we can't help but justify, even laud, our own actions. When making a judgment of others we are naturally more critical. And when that very judgment is made out of the audible range of that person, our findings may border on the harsh.

The "I-You-He" game demonstrates the human tendency to muddy our evaluations with our feelings. It is only when we have clear and proper definitions of "brave," "foolhardy" and "reckless" that we can make judgments without getting the sub-jective and objective mixed up.

Let's clarify our paradigm further by attempting to articulate definitions for these terms and the distinctions inherent in their comparison. This is but one example of the kind of process in which a white belt intellectual needs to become proficient.

So, what is the definition of "brave"? I think that we would all agree, for example, that rushing into a burning building to save trapped children is a courageous act. So, a brave person might well be defined as someone who takes a necessary risk for a noble purpose.

What then is "foolhardy"? Well, if the individual rushing into the burning building could douse himself with water first or put on a smoke mask in order to increase his own chances of sur-vival, and doesn't, then he is taking an unnecessary risk. Even though he is acting impulsively and foolishly, at least he is doing it in order to save lives. So, a foolhardy person could be defined as someone who takes an unnecessary risk for a noble purpose.

If that same individual rushes into a burning building just to watch the beams fall down, he's taking a totally unnecessary risk for no worthwhile purpose. That is called "reckless" behavior.

These definitions force everyone — even Steve — to agree that anyone driving through city streets at 85 miles an hour to make a meeting is engaging in behavior that can only be described as purely "reckless." He is taking an unnecessary risk with his own life and the lives of others for no significant reason.

The reason this "I-You-He" game is so important is because it is a game that is constantly being played all around us. "Brave — foolhardy — reckless" is just one example; there are count-less others.

Let's get practical

You should be able to come up with dozens of these groupings on your own. Creating them helps you sharpen their distinctions and helps accustom you to the overall need for utilizing coherent and reasoned definitions.

Exercise

Replace the "?" in column 3 with the most appropriate words:

I AM	YOU ARE	HE IS
Generous	Loose with money	?
Determined	Obsessed	?
Strong-willed	Stubborn	?
An educator	A persuader	?

Answers:

- *A spendthrift*
- *A fanatic*
- *Pig-headed*
- *A brain-washer*

Of course, some groupings are of particular significance and not just examples of basic semantic differentiations.

Let's look at two such sets in the following altercation. The definitions needed in these groupings are vital because these concepts are ever-present in the process of learning and accepting new ideas.

> *A father and son are arguing about an important decision in the boy's life. The discussion gets heated and at one point the father yells at his son: "You're just a stubborn mule."*
>
> *The son yells back, "You just can't admit that I'm strong-willed."*
>
> *The boy slams the door and on his way out mutters, "He's just trying to brainwash me."*
>
> *The father overhears the remark and shouts after him, "Brainwash?! I'm just trying to educate you!"*

In this most typical scene, who is right — the father or the son? Is the father an "educator," as he says he is, or is he a "brain-washer," as the son thinks? What about the boy? Is he "stubborn" or "strong-willed"?

The answers, of course, can be found in the working definitions of these terms.

- An "educator" is someone who imparts all the evidence available on any particular topic, seriously entertains all questions, and encourages you to use your mind to arrive at an independent conclusion. An educator says, "Here is the evidence. Check it out. Think for yourself."

- A "persuader," on the other hand, has an agenda. He focuses your attention on the information as he sees it. He doesn't encourage you to check out all the facts and reach an independent conclusion. A persuader says, "Here is all the evidence you need. You can trust my interpretation."

- A "brain-washer," on the "third hand," uses emotional appeal instead of facts, especially when he fears the facts won't stand up to determined scrutiny. A brain-washer says (often at the top of his lungs), "Forget the evidence! Rely on me. I wouldn't mislead you, would I?"

The contrasts are self-evident.

Let's try another set.

- *Stong-willed*
- *Stubborn*
- *Pig-headed*

- A "strong-willed" person is someone who is willing to consider what the other person has to say but won't be easily bamboozled. A strong-willed person says, "If you have evidence, put it on the table. Don't yell at me, don't bully me, and don't try to seduce me. Just stick to the facts."

- What is "stubborn"? A stubborn person has difficulty reconsidering his position even in the face of the strongest evidence. He says, "I heard all your proofs, but I still think you're wrong, and I don't want to discuss it any further."

- What is "pig-headed"? That's someone who refuses to even look at the evidence. He says, "I don't need to hear what you have to say. I know that I'm right! That's it!"

In the world of ideas and beliefs, people will often try to bully you and seduce you, and it takes a strong-willed person to stand up to that. People can twist anything to suit their point of view, but you are less likely to be their victim if you can clearly see whether they are showing you real evidence, pushing you to their conclusions, or pitching an emotional appeal.

Use the above definitions when you have discussions with people. If someone challenges you and tells you, "You're wrong," then ask the person, "Why should I agree with you? What evidence do you have to back up your position?" If he says, "You were brainwashed," ask him, "What was I taught that is wrong? Show me why you think my opinion ignores the evidence."

The more clarity you have, the harder it is for someone to confuse you.

That's being an intellectual. With your white belt, the definitions are always leading the way — making sure you are using your mind to see your way through life, rather than muddling your way through based on feelings alone.

Define. Define. Define.

Let's face it — we all hide.

A difficult situation arises, the pressure is on, and we go into hiding, each of us in our own favorite ways.

One of the more common forms of hiding is in language. You don't know how to say "No" to somebody, so you hide instead.

"I'll try" is a good substitute.

"I'll let you know" is another one.

"Let me sleep on it" is a fairly effective dodge.

You probably have your own tried and proven methods of screening your true intentions, but some concealment is universal. And we're so used to it that we hardly realize we're doing it.

Aren't we all guilty of saying, "I can't do it," when we really mean to say, "I don't want to do it"? Don't you frequently say, "I know," when "I think so" would be far more accurate? Instead of saying, "I'll try," might you sometimes say too hastily, "I will"?

An orange belt intellectual is more advanced than a white belt intellectual. With a white belt, you understand the need for clear definitions. With an orange belt, you insist on using them. The orange belt intellectual only says exactly what he means. He doesn't just define his terms, he utilizes them.

▶ "Calling All Atheists..."

One of the most important issues in life is the existence of God. The storied history of this debate is known to all, and this is not the place to review, resume, or resolve the greatest of all questions. But precisely because of its import, the definitions of the terms used in the arguments are especially significant.

There are probably tens of thousands, if not millions of people in this country alone, who call themselves "atheists." Now, an "atheist" is someone who "knows" that God does not exist. And, you would probably agree, anyone who "knows" anything should have at least some evidence to support his "knowledge." Naturally, finding evidence, even thin evidence, that something does not exist is nearly impossible. So, use of the term "atheist," in any context, is a great example of something no bona fide orange belt intellectual would do.

Even the term "agnostic," which is probably the term they really want to use in describing themselves, implies a "knowledge" that you cannot know if there really is a God. Webster's defines "agnostic" as: "of or relating to the belief that the existence of any ultimate reality (as God) is unknown and probably unknowable."

Again, evidence of some kind, even for this claim, does not exist. It is far more accurate and honest for them to dispense with the labels and just say that they really don't know if God exists or not. Or, they might more accurately state that they simply choose to trust what certain professors, mentors, or authors have told them. That's what a true, above-board, orange belt intellectual would do.

Watch what you're saying!

The power contained within this level is such that the process of becoming really careful about saying what you mean forces you to honestly assess your most personal beliefs and attitudes in life. As just stated, a self-proclaimed "atheist" may come to a realization that what he thought he "knew,"he didn't.

Similarly, if someone goes through life thinking of himself as "happy," he now must face the necessity of knowing exactly what that means! What is "happy"? How can I know if I really am "happy"? What is the definition?

One possible definition of happiness is "taking pleasure in what one has." Employing this definition, the person pondering this question can consider, "Am I at this moment getting satisfaction from the fact that I am healthy, I have a family that loves me, and I have enough money to fulfill my immediate needs?" Upon reflection, the person might realize that he is not really experiencing full pleasure in what he or she currently has, because in reality he is focusing on certain desires that have yet to be fulfilled.

The orange belt intellectual may well come to the realization that rather than taking pleasure in what he has, he is really stuck commiserating about what he does not have. What this person should say is that he is really "just surviving." Practically speaking, if a person does not use definitions as a tool in thinking issues through, he will never know if he is aiming his life on target. Such a person may never discover that there exists a level of happiness out there that far exceeds the one he is currently experiencing. How tragic...

"What's it like?"

Such a person is like the child in the following fable:

A king was walking through a forest one day and noticed that many of the trees had targets with bull's eyes painted on them. Incredibly, every single bull's eye had an arrow embedded right through it.

The king was so impressed with this display of marksmanship that he sent out a search party to find the archer. Up ahead, they discovered a 10-year-old boy walking with bows and arrows in his pouch. Upon encountering the lad, the king asked disbelievingly, "Are you responsible for all these bull's eyes?"

"Yes," the boy replied.

This pleased the king greatly and he immediately asked the boy to train all his soldiers to shoot with similar accuracy. "It's really no big deal," the boy said. "Anyone can do it. I'll show you."

The boy took out an arrow and fired it into a tree. He then picked up a paintbrush, walked over to the tree and proceeded to paint a target around the arrow. Result? Bull's eye! Every time!

Living without using definitions is like first shooting an arrow and then painting the target around it. We just assume that what we do or feel is on target. We feel that we are "good," so we guess we are. We feel like we are truly "happy," so we guess we are.

In summary, with "orange" on your belt, you not only have definitions for things like goodness and happiness, you also check with those definitions before making statements about your thoughts or feelings.

Take a deep breath. You are about to take a giant leap forward on the "intellectual" continuum. And you may want to keep a mirror handy, because climbing to the "red belt intellectual" rung requires that you a take a good, hard look at yourself.

Chances are that amidst all the strengths, weaknesses, and personality quirks you've cultivated over the years, you might have also discovered a contradiction or two.

- You fully recognize the importance of a healthy diet, yet your meal regimen is peppered with donuts, London broil, and deep-fried onions.

- It's clear to you that it is better to be happy than wealthy, but you spend a good share of your "leisure" time working — like over 60 precent of Americans who, while on vacation, "check-in" with the office several times a day.

- The coughing is getting worse, your breathing is labored, your clothes stink, and the kids have stopped talking to you — but the smoking must go on.

How are we supposed to understand this irrational behavior of ours? So much of what we actually do just defies reason!

The red belt intellectual has no need for explanations. He simply does not participate is these deeds of inconsistency. He looks in the mirror and says, "I will act according to my beliefs." He not only says what he means, he takes it a step further: he means what he says.

Qualitatively, he has entered a totally new arena of awareness and action. He is now making certain that his feelings are totally guided by what he believes and not the reverse. The problem for most people is that while they understand something to be true, they haven't really connected their ideas to their emotions. And people whose feelings are disconnected from their convictions can be said to actually be "anti-intellectual."

On the "red belt" level, a person's understanding begins to directly influence his feelings, desires, and actions. There is no place, therefore, for incongruity and contradiction. His actions are now totally in sync with what he believes and feels. And when those dimensions come together in harmonious fashion, the satisfaction is beyond words.

An illustration

Let's return for a moment to our smoking example.

If you ask most smokers if smoking is dangerous, they'll probably say, "Yes."

If you then ask them, "Would you ever knowingly do something that you knew was dangerous and could possibly kill you?", they'd probably say, "Of course not."

Now if you say, "So tell me, if you know smoking is dangerous and you wouldn't do something dangerous, why do you smoke?", they'll probably respond by saying, "I know it's harmful, but I feel like smoking anyway."

Most smokers are intellectually aware that smoking increases the risk of lung cancer, emphysema, and heart disease. But the smoker's desire to smoke obscures that reality, making him rationalize away the danger. His understanding does not translate into feelings or actions. Often, but not always, it is only a major dose of reality, like a heart attack, that will make him quit. So powerful is the resistance that even a major crisis is frequently not convincing enough. The self-destruction must continue.

The red belt intellectual internalizes the knowledge of the dangers of smoking long before he would succumb to a heart attack. He takes what he understands so seriously that it actually determines what he feels and does, and not vice versa.

Let's get practical

When the red belt intellectual comes to the realization that something is true, if he has accepted a fact intellectually, then he is prepared to act on this basis. It is not just an intellectual concept, it is a reality, and he is consistent in his beliefs, speech, and actions.

This means that if you really believe that happiness is more important than money, then you would do whatever is necessary to learn how to be happy (yes, even if it costs you some money). In this category, it is not enough to know your terms and to use them appropriately; you've got to be ready to act.

You will know you have reached this stage when you find the time and the discipline to assess your beliefs and to plan your life according to them. A few minutes every night is all you really need.

Ask yourself:

- *What did I accomplish today?*

- *Am I satisfied with that?*

- *Why? Why not?*

- *Were my actions fully consistent with my belief system?*

- *What mistakes did I make?*

- *How can I correct them?*

Sage wisdom

The Sages of the Talmud have taught us, "If you see a student of wisdom transgressing at night, do not think badly of him in the morning, for surely he has already repented" (*Berachos* 19a).

This implies that a wise man, a red belt intellectual, understands that he should use his intellect for living. He knows he is making some mistakes so he takes a serious inventory to get himself in touch with reality. When he realizes that he missed something somewhere, he makes a plan to ensure that the mistake does not repeat itself. He is taking charge of his life.

He is now ready to climb the ladder again!

Brown belt intellectual

The transition from red belt to brown belt is subtle, but its implications can be dramatic. It is the difference between being reactive and proactive.

The red belt intellectual realizes that to really live life effectively he has to use his mind constantly to guide him. He recognizes his mistakes and adjusts accordingly. The brown belt intellectual is not satisfied with that. He plans ahead. He sees the big picture. He figures out what he wants to accomplish first, and formulates the best possible approach to reach those goals.

For example, instead of instantly reacting to his children's misbehaving, he asks himself, "What do I want to accomplish with my children?" You won't find a brown belt intellectual yelling at his kids since he knows it doesn't work. He first focuses on his goal: "My goal is to communicate to my daughter to shut the screen door behind her when she walks in, without making her feel bad." He will then figure out an effective course of action to reach his goal. He might tell his daughter: "If you remember to shut the screen door ten times, I'll take you out for an ice cream sundae." Or something like that.

He uses his mind like you would use a flashlight, guiding him out of the darkness into reality. It is the beacon that not only directs his path, but also creates it.

Proactive in three ways

The brown belt intellectual clarifies beforehand what he wants to do and how he wants to do it. And he does this in three different ways.

1. He constantly asks himself, "What am I doing and why?" Too often, people are just zombies, falling into routines of behavior that have never really been successful or satisfying. Ask them why they do what they do in the particular way they do it, and they stutter and stammer their way through some flimsy explanation. Why? Because they have no real idea if they are accomplishing what they set out to do and if this is really the best way to do it.

   The brown belt intellectual, as in the example with the screen door above, first clarifies his goal before deciding on a course of action. When you think about it, it's obvious that this is the most prudent strategy. But that's the catch; you have to "think" about it.

2. The brown belt never forgets that he is not living to work; he is working to live! Sure, he cares about his business schedule, but he cares about his life much more. If he is going to plan 9 to 5, he will not neglect to plan 5 to 9 as well.

When he comes home from work, he might decide to simply mow the lawn, work out, or be a couch potato. The difference is that he does it consciously. He decides if he wants to accomplish something in his spare time, enjoy his family and friends, or just "veg out."

He plans his day by asking serious questions about his motivations.

- *Shall I read the newspaper or write that uncomfortable e-mail tonight? Why? If I want to be well-informed, how much time should I spend doing it?*

- *Do I really want to improve my marriage or my relationships? What's the best way to do that?*

- *Do I want to broaden my interests? Music? Religion? Sports? What's the best way to do that?*

The brown belt intellectual doesn't want to wake up every morning in a foul mood, groaning about the day ahead of him. He wants to be fresh, invigorated and shouting, "It's great tobe alive!" — which, of course, is quite possible — if he plans ahead.

3. This constant self-evaluation is not limited to his day-to-day activities. The brown belt extends this scrutiny to life goals as well. He ignores neither the micro nor the macro. He asks:

- *What is the purpose of existence?*

- *What are my strengths and weaknesses? How do I work on them?*

- *Do I have a particular role in creation? What might it be?*

- *What might I be willing to die for? How do I make sure that I also live for it?*

He is constantly refining the "big picture" — aligning his goals with his deepest and most meaningful desires.

He is functioning as a genuine intellectual — aware, clear, honest, and planning ahead.

He is ready for the final leap — the "black belt"!

Black belt intellectual

The black belt intellectual lives in the ultimate reality: with the constant awareness of God's Presence.

As we discussed in stage five of our chapter on Free Will, the highest level of understanding your potential on this world is being in touch with the aspirations of your soul. The brown belt intellectual ponders his life's purpose by asking soul-related questions. It follows that the black belt intellectual not only asks these questions, he is in continual and persistent contemplation of his role vis-a-vis God Himself.

After a brief recess, God is back in vogue ("Thank God."). As affluence became more and more present in Western society, affluence soon became "Omnipresent." Money replaced God in many circles and the new worship was just as intense and vigorous as "the old one."

And while prosperity and material comfort continue to remain essential goals for most of us out there, spirituality is clearly making a comeback. The transparent vacuity of the physical world, along with its tawdry trappings, have created a renewed thirst for godliness and meaning in people's lives. The media is inundated with books, news specials, documentaries, and feature films that spotlight, both overtly and through metaphor, "Man's Search for Meaning."

Apologizing for or hiding one's religious belief system is no longer required. And the black belt intellectual epitomizes this resurgence. He never loses sight of what his life is really about. His actions are in complete concert with his goals. He knows that God is with him, constantly teaching, loving, and guiding him through the angst and complexities of life.

Black belt intellectuals come to a realization of who they are. They not only contemplate their place in the world, they understand it — and then they live it!

As a result of this awareness and constant focus, they are more complete people. Their work is more meaningful and goal-directed. Their relationships are more satisfying because they know exactly what they want. They can take without feeling guilty because their self-esteem is rock solid. And they can give with sincerity and a lack of pretension.

Years ago, the movie "Star Wars" made popular the phrase, "May the Force be with you!" The world seems to be returning to that belief. "The Almighty is with you!" And when we remember to keep that perspective ever-present, we connect with the Ultimate Power available to us. The potential is limitless.

If you're a black belt intellectual, you know that God is your Father in Heaven. You don't need another Sinai-like revelation to prove it. The design of the world and all its complexities is more than enough proof for you. The tiny miracles of everyday life are constant reminders of His presence. You know that He is always with you, and you perceive Him watching over you and saying, "My child, let's go together." That's living with ultimate meaning. And that's power. That's when the black belt intellectual is accessing the highest power of the intellect.

Let's review

A person who thinks straight, without being confused by feelings, is called an intellectual. He leads with his head, not with his heart. Mastering the art of becoming a true intellectual and reaching the pinnacle of intellectual command must be an incremental process. Each "belt," signifying a deeper appreciation of the intellectual progression, must be acquired one at a time, in order to realize the full potency of the skills attained.

- **White Belt:** gets definitions; doesn't rely on emotions to make decisions.

- **Orange Belt:** uses the definitions he has attained; says what he means.

- **Red Belt:** uses his understanding to influence his feelings; means what he says.

- **Brown Belt:** lives what he means on a day-to-day basis; plans ahead.

- **Black Belt:** uses his mind to live with the constant reality of God beside him.

7 LOVE

"Love makes the world go 'round."
"Love is a many splendored thing."
"All you need is love."

Love.

Has there ever been a greater mystery?

Is there anyone who doesn't yearn to learn the secrets of love?

Can a formula for love really be created?

What do Judaism and the Bible say about love?

The first and perhaps most puzzling thing we need to understand about love is that Judaism does not treat love as an ideal, a conviction, a principle, a beautiful concept, or an unfamed passion. It is an obligation. A duty. A responsibility. A requirement.

Yes, you may read that again. Despite everything you've ever seen, felt, heard, or believed about the splendor, allure, fascination, and magic of love...bottom line is — it's an obligation.

Now, don't get turned off. The fact that Judaism sees love as an obligation does not mean that it has no magic, allure, or fascination. It has all of that, and more! Love has an infinite amount of intrigue and power, but primarily it is an obligation.

- *Where does this come from?*
- *What does this mean?*

Here is what the Bible says: "Love your neighbor as yourself, I am God" (*Leviticus* 19:18).

Let us examine this key concept in greater depth and, in the process, we will uncover some of the greatest secrets in how to achieve a really successful and satisfying relationship.

▶ The Questions...

God instructs, indeed commands us, to love each other. And while doing so, He surrounds the commandment with seemingly extraneous information. This prompts us to do what Jews do best — ask questions.

The above verse is one of over 5,000 verses in the Bible; and it is one of the most compelling. Read it again and see if you are bothered by the same perplexities that trouble us.

1. How can "love" possibly be an obligation? Either you love someone or you don't. Who ever heard of legislating an emotion?! It's not something you can obligate someone to do.
2. The same verse in the Bible that obligates us to love one another also says: "Don't take revenge and don't bear a grudge." What does taking revenge or bearing a grudge have to do with loving your neighbor? What are these commandments doing together in the same verse?
3. Why does the verse say, "...love your neighbor as yourself"? The Bible never uses extra words, so what is the phrase "as yourself" coming to add?
4. The original Hebrew words, *v'ahavta l're'acha*, which most often are translated in English as "love your neighbor," should really be translated, "love your friend." Why does the Bible refer to our neighbor as our "friend"?

5. The verse ends with the words, "I am God." What does this have to do with loving your friend?

Answering these five questions will open a virtual treasure chest in our perpetual quest for understanding what love really is and how we can acquire it.

At first blush, the thought of obligating any emotion seems absurd, if not impossible. Demanding that someone "feel" anything appears to be totally antithetical to what sensations are all about. And yet, if God instructs us to do so, it must be possible.

It is.

Consider the following example:

You have two children — a girl, age 6, and a boy, age 9. One day you walk into the house and hear loud voices. Your son's voice is loudest, so naturally you summon him to the den.

> *"Hey…what's all the yelling about?" you ask.*
> *"I hate my sister" is the reply. "I hate her, hate her, hate her!!"*

What do you think your most likely response to this outburst might be?

> *Well, I can understand that. If you hate her, you hate her. It's a feeling, so I guess it's okay. What's for dinner tonight?*

Idiocy!

You would do nothing of the sort! You'd probably say what most parents say at times like that:

> *Don't talk that way! You have to love your sister!*

Whereupon he is likely to reply:

> *But I'm only telling you the truth. You want me to lie? How can I love that little brat? I really hate her.*

And in case you should inquire as to why he hates his sister, you may hear:

> *"Because she took the bigger piece of cake." Or, "She took my eraser without asking me." "She moved my chair." (You have to have kids to appreciate this.)*

Now, if this goes on for long, you're likely to lose your temper. You won't stand for it. You'll say:

That's the reason you hate your sister?! That's nonsense! You have to love your sister!

You're not simply suggesting that the brother love his sister; you're *demanding* it. Between brothers and sisters, love is not something that's just preferable; it is something we expect. Nothing in the world should get in the way of their love.

So not only is demanding love not impossible, it's actually something that most of us are used to doing all the time. Moreover, it is precisely by accepting upon ourselves the obligation to love someone that we begin to understand the process of how to love.

Recall, if you will, the example from the Five Levels of Pleasure (see pp. 39-41). Parents, even before their children are born, are naturally committed to loving their children, and are therefore determined to focus primarily on what is good about their child.

The real question is, however: How can we activate this process in all of our relationships — to be able to love "at will"? In order to do that we need to become consciously aware of the dynamics which take place within a person who accepts the obligation to love.

To begin to understand this better, let's contrast the definition of love as seen by the Jewish people versus Western civilization's view of love.

Judaism defines love as: the emotional pleasure a human being experiences when he understands and focuses on the virtues of another human being.

The emotion of love, therefore, is overwhelmingly dependent on how one views another person. If we choose to focus on people's virtues, we will love them. If we choose to focus on their deficiencies, we will dislike them.

[Not as simple as it sounds, but not as complicated as you might think.]

This explains how the Bible can obligate us to love someone. The way we choose to view other people is completely within our control. To attain the feeling of love, we are obligated by the Bible to focus on another person's virtues. By extension, we will love them. And the more intimately we know someone and his virtues, the deeper our love will become.

Western culture, on the other hand, is heavily influenced by secular ideologies, in this case, the Greek concept of love — Cupid. You know the story. Cupid flits around with his wings, shoots a man and a woman with an arrow, and — presto! — they're in love.

This concept of love dominates the Western world. It deludes us into believing that love is a mystical "happening." You don't work on loving people. It either happens or it doesn't.

In Western consciousness, love is a stroke of "fate." There's no rhyme or reason. There's no effort involved. Love is not based on commitment or on any deep understanding of the person that you love.

In Greek style/American style love, two people "fall" in love and get married. They just "happen" to "fall" in love — as if they were victims. Loving someone is not really a choice at all! So, if you want to stay married, all you can do is hope and pray that Cupid doesn't shoot you again! It's no surprise that this philosophy has produced a society with a divorce rate of over 50 percent.

The Jewish outlook, on the other hand, is that love is based upon the *understanding* and *appreciation* of another's virtues. When people are truly committed to focusing on each other's virtues, they won't "fall" out of love. This is exactly why so few people completely abandon their kids.

Ask a parent:

> *"Did your children ever keep you up all night,*
> *whooping and coughing, and driving you batty?"*
> *"Yes."*
> *"Did you ever lose your temper and think, 'I'd*
> *love to strangle this little monster?'"*
> *"Well, occasionally, it did happen, I'm only*
> *human."*
> *"Do you still love your kids?"*
> *"Of course, I love my kids."*

No parent ever gets up in the morning and says, "I'm not giving you breakfast because you kept me up last night."

We don't stop caring about our children just because they annoy us. We don't "fall out of love" with our kids, because we understand that loving our children isn't just a "happening." It's a responsibility that we are committed to from the time they're born. We know their virtues because as parents we accept the obligation to love them despite the aggravation.

> *If we would only carry that same commitment into our marriages and friendships, we would all be a lot better off.*

There are actually three separate commandments contained within one verse:

- *Don't take revenge,*

- *Don't bear a grudge, and*

- *Love your neighbor as yourself.*

Why are these three commandments in the same verse? What does one have to do with the other?

Their placement is not at all accidental or incidental. In juxtaposing these commands, the Bible is revealing yet another secret of how to love.

If you train yourself not to try to "even the score" by taking revenge, then you won't bother to remember wrongs people do to you, and thus you won't be bearing a grudge. Then all that remains for you to focus on are the good things. Nothing negative will be holding you back from seeing the merits and loving the other person.

In other words, the road is now clear for you to pay careful attention to perfecting the love formula — understanding and focusing on the virtues of another human being.

Love your neighbor "as yourself"?

Say you're slicing some Muenster cheese and you accidentally cut your finger. Would you take revenge by grabbing the knife and cutting your other hand? After all, it was your other hand that perpetrated the offense, was it not??

Of course not. Your other hand is as much a part of you as anything else. Revenge would be insane!

When we learn to appreciate that we are all truly united, then hurting the other guy by "paying him back" is as ridiculous as hurting yourself. That's why the Bible says: Love your neighbor "as yourself." If I realize that the other guy and I are really part of the very same unit, then revenge is as silly as cutting my other hand with the knife.

Now, all this unity talk may sound to you like pie in the sky, but, in fact, this is what the Almighty really wants for us. This state of harmony somehow continues to elude us, and we, as a people, are sinking deeper and deeper into the abyss of dissension and cacophony. It's sad.

More often than not, it takes conflict or war against a common enemy to bring this message home to the human race. History bears this out all too painfully.

You need look no further than the aftermath of the World Trade Center terror attack to see this point clearly. Citizens around the country, in short order, cast aside petty differences in favor of rallying around the President and democracy. Coalitions of every color, race, and creed imaginable formed on local, national, and international fronts. Political allegiance and previous bias were no match for the bourgeoning super-patriotism wrought upon us by our enemies. Such is the power of unity when we need it.

Similar phenomena have been recorded throughout time, as God must periodically resort to the most painful of avenues to bring the messages of togetherness to the fore. How much healthier and more prudent would it be, if only mankind learned this lesson on its own — without the agonizing Divine intervention.

Parents *naturally* relate this way to their children. No matter how badly children misbehave, parents don't stop loving them. Annoyance? Yes. Reprimand? Of course. But normal parents don't take revenge on their own children. They don't bear a grudge, because they relate to their children as an extension of themselves; so hurting our children is really hurting ourselves. Since parents don't desire revenge, they're able to forget the bad things and focus on the good. That's why it's easy for parents to love their children.

This very same dynamic can work with *any* relationship! With parents and children, the process is more instinctive. But when it comes to marriage, the potential for oneness is even greater! Unlike the parent/child affiliation, spouses actually *choose* each other, allowing for the prospects for enhanced unity to be even greater! But it does take a lot more work...naturally.

The Hebrew word *re'acha,* "your friend," conveys more accurately than "your neighbor" that we're really in this together; we're on the same side. And that's the feeling everyone should have about everyone else.

Of course, friendship, like love, is another theme that has been extensively reflected upon. And the two topics are inexorably connected to one another. Gaining a deeper understanding in the dynamics of friendship can also help us in our odyssey to know and attain real love.

The following two stories about friendship, taken from Jewish folklore, lend clarity to the meaning of friendship and love. The first one helps us answer question number four, and the second one helps us with the final question. Together they speak volumes about the ingredients of love and why God places such a premium on loving one another.

> *There was once a father and son who were discussing the topic of friendship.*
>
> *The father said, "You know, son, it's tough to make friends."*
>
> *The son said, "What do you mean, Dad? I have lots of friends."*
>
> *"How many friends do you have," the father asked?*

The son thought for a long while and said, "I've counted them up. I must have two hundred friends!"

"Two hundred friends? A young man like you?" said the father. "That's amazing. I can't believe it."

"Why, Dad? How many friends do you have?"

"Me? My whole life I've worked really hard at it and I've only achieved half a friend."

"But Dad, everybody likes you. You're a wonderful man. What are you talking about — only half a friend? And what is half a friend, anyway?"

"Look son, you have to know whether your friends are really your friends. A friend in need is a friend indeed. Why don't you test it out and see if your friends are really friends?"

The father had an idea. Since this story may have taken place during the Roman occupation of Israel, over 2,000 years ago, you need to know that the Romans were especially stringent about law and order. If they caught a murderer or a thief, they would mete out swift and harsh judgment. And they did the same to anyone thought to be an accomplice to the crime. They meant business.

"Here's what you do," the father suggested. "A goat's blood resembles human blood. Take a goat, slaughter it and put it in a sack. Then, at night, go to your friends and say, 'You've got to help me. I went to a bar last night and had a little too much to drink. There was a guy there who started insulting me and we got into an argument. He took a swing at me, I took a swing back at him, the fight rolled into the street, and I hit him a little too hard and killed him. Now I've got to get rid of the body. Otherwise I'm a dead duck.' Then ask your friends to help you get rid of the body."

The son thought it was a great idea and he tried it out. Night after night, he took the sack of goat meat around to all his friends. It took him a couple of weeks and a few goats, but he got through his two hundred friends.

As you might guess, *not one* wanted anything to do with him. They understood that *he* wasn't responsible, that the *other* fellow started the fight, but they didn't want any part of it.

> *Finally, the son came back to his father and said, "Dad, I guess you're right. My friends aren't such good friends. How about your half a friend? Maybe he'll help."*
>
> *The father said, "Sure, try him out. Go to his house, and tell him you're Chaim's son. Tell him what happened, and see whether he helps you."*
>
> *That night the son knocked at his father's friend's door.*
>
> *"Who's there?" a frightened voice asked.*
>
> *"It's Chaim's son."*
>
> *"Oh, Chaim's son! Come in. What can I do for you?"*

The son told him the whole story about the bar and the fight and the body.

> *"Well, really, I shouldn't help you, but you're Chaim's son, what can I do?"*

He took the boy out in the backyard. They dug a hole and buried the sack.

> *"Now go back home. Stay out of the bars. If somebody insults you, just keep quiet. But most of all, forget you ever met me."*
>
> *The son went back to his father and said, "Dad, why do you call him half a friend? He's the only one who helped me!"*
>
> *"What did he say to you?"*
>
> *"He said, 'Really, I shouldn't help you, but you're Chaim's son, what can I do?'"*
>
> *"That's half a friend," said the father. "Somebody who pauses and says, 'Really I shouldn't do this,' that's half a friend."*
>
> *"Then Dad, what's a real friend?"*

So, his father told him this next story (cited in *Shtei Yados*), which will help us answer our last question.

> *Two young men had grown up together and become very close friends. They were living at a time when the Roman Empire was split into two parts — one half controlled by an emperor in Rome and the other half ruled by an emperor in Syria. After each of the friends married, one moved to Rome and the other moved to Syria. Together they started an import-export business, and though they lived far apart, they remained very close friends.*
>
> *One time, when the fellow from Rome was visiting in Syria, someone accused him of being a spy for Rome and plotting against the emperor. He was an innocent man — it was just a vicious rumor. So, they brought him to the Syrian emperor, and he was subsequently sentenced to death.*
>
> *When he was being led out to his execution, he was asked if he had any last requests. The accused man pleaded: "Please, I'm an innocent man, but I can't prove it. So, if I'm going to die, at least let me go back to Rome first, settle my affairs, and say good-bye to my family. They don't know my business, like who owes me money, where all my goods are. Let me just go back to Rome, put my affairs in order, and then I'll come back and you can execute me."*
>
> *The emperor laughed at him. "What are you, crazy? You think we'd let you go? What possible guarantee will we have that you're going to come back?"*
>
> *The Jew said, "Wait. I have a friend here in Syria who will stand in for me. He'll be my guarantor. If I don't come back, you can kill him instead."*

The emperor was intrigued. "This I've got to see. Okay, bring in your friend."

The fellow from Syria was called in. Sure enough, he agreed without hesitation to take the Roman Jew's place in prison, and to be killed in his stead if the friend did not return.

The emperor was so startled by this arrangement that he agreed to let the Roman Jew go. "I'll give you sixty days. Put your affairs in order. If you're not back by dawn of the sixtieth day, your friend is dead."

Off went the Roman Jew, racing back to his family to say good-bye and to put his affairs in order. After a lot of tears and good-byes, he started back in plenty of time before the sixty days were up.

Those were the days of sailing galleys, and sometimes you could sit for days waiting for the right wind to come up. As luck would have it, there was no wind for several days, the sailboat was delayed, and by the time the Jew arrived in Syria, dawn of the sixtieth day was breaking.

As agreed, the jailers took out the fellow from Syria for the execution.

In those days, an execution was a gala affair, and early in the morning the crowds began to gather. Finally, as they were just about to perform the execution, the fellow from Rome came running in. "Wait! Stop! I'm back. Don't kill him. I'm the real prisoner!"

The executioner let the fellow from Syria go and was about to take the Jew from Rome in his place. "Wait a minute," the reprieved guarantor argued. "You can't kill him. His time limit was up. I'm the guarantor. You've got to kill me instead!"

The two friends were equally adamant. "Kill me instead!" "No, kill me!" The executioner didn't

know what to do. The crowd was in an uproar,
watching them fight it out.

Finally, the emperor stepped in. In wonder and
amazement, he turned to the two of them and said,
"I'll let both of you go free on one condition — that
you make me your third friend!"

That's friendship. That's true unity.

That's why the same verse that says, "Love your neighbor," also says "I am God." Unity and friendship among God's children are so precious that God says, so to speak, "If you love each other, I want to be your third friend." This means that if we're united, we have the power of God behind us.

Unity is so precious to God that even when we are not as good as we should be, our unity allows us to achieve far more than any one holy, talented, or great individual could possibly achieve alone. In sports, we call it "teamwork." Teams with unusual self-lessness and chemistry often topple opponents with greater raw skill and power.

In life, we call it "love."

We see examples of this in Jewish history. Ahab — despite the fact that he was an evil king — was more successful in battle than any other king the Jewish people ever had. Why? Because he benefited from exceptional unity among the Jewish populace. God granted the Jews military success, despite the sinister intentions of their leader. Unity is the quality God wants most for all His children. Simply put, when we are united, God is our "third friend."

Infighting and strife among us is therefore our most insidious and debilitating enemy. Disharmony prevents us from being a predominant force, and reduces us to an impotent collection of self-absorbed individuals.

If we're united, the Almighty is with us. If we're divided, we're on our own.

It's called "The Power of Love."

EPILOGUE

Hopefully you are not one of those readers who cannot stand the suspense of waiting for the end of a book and simply jumps ahead to the epilogue. Instead, you have trekked from the Introduction all the way through "Love," and are ready to put your newfound wisdom into practice.

- You understand that God is perfect and therefore needs nothing from Man. He created you for your **Pleasure** — all five incredible levels of it.

- You recognize that **Prayer** is a phenomenally powerful vehicle that keeps you aware of the Creator at all times and helps you to constantly reassess your needs and priorities in life. It is certainly not for "Him." It is your chance to develop a truly authentic relationship with God.

- You know that truth is indeed quite attainable — and that **Knowledge,** belief, faith, and socialization are four very different categories of certainty. It really does matter how you know what you know.

- You appreciate that appreciating what you have is the secret to real **Happiness.** But DOING IT is quite another story. Practicing the pleasure-count, and listing and prioritizing your blessings is the best recipe for attaining maximum happiness.

- You value the energy that **Free Will** can give you and can comprehend the five steps necessary to mastering the awesome potential that free will contains. You are ready to make decisions actively and can distinguish between cravings of the body and aspirations of the soul.

- You realize that a bona fide **Intellectual** leads with his head not with his heart. By acquiring each "belt" on the intellectual scale, you are able to get definitions, say what you mean, mean what you say, live what you mean and constantly dwell in God's reality.

- And finally, you grasp the power of what real **Love** can accomplish. With unity, the force of God Himself is always with us.

So...now what?

It is true. Achieving mastery of these seven keys can bring you to the threshold of greater fulfillment in life. But where does religion fit into the mix? Why does Judaism, particularly, contain the very best framework for applying these principles into your daily life? And how do you get started?

▸ The eighth key

We have described seven essential foundations of life in this book, but, as you probably know, this list is hardly exhaustive. In fact, there is one critical component that we have omitted. And it is a veritable prerequisite to your capacity to fully put these concepts into practice.

An incident that happened to me several years ago best illustrates the impact of this most crucial construct.

I was walking in Boro Park one afternoon and happened to pass a synagogue. (Hardly unusual — practically every block in Boro Park has one.) As I pass the shul, an elderly gentleman is standing outside and he approaches me. I had never seen him before.

> *"Are you going into the shul for the funeral?" he asks.*
> *"No," I respond. "I didn't know there was a funeral inside."*
> *"Well, why don't you stop in anyway?"*
> *"Any particular reason why I should go in to a funeral I know nothing about?" I inquired.*

(I had never been invited to a funeral before.)

> *"Of course," he said, "it's Mr. Schachner's funeral."*
> *"I don't...er...didn't know any Mr. Schachner,"*
> *I advised him while continuing my stride past the shul.*

But the stranger, strangely persisted.

> *"Of course you know him," he pleaded.*

I turned around.

> *"And how would you know if I knew him — you don't even know me!" I posed.*

For some reason, my new friend then began to tell me details about Mr. Schachner — residence, occupation, family, etc. — in a seemingly desperate attempt to get me inside the synagogue! Included in the biography were the names of two of his married daughters. Obviously their names were no longer Schachner and, as it turns out, he was right! I did know them. I just hadn't heard that their father had passed away.

Naturally, I turned around and went inside.

The sanctuary was dimly lit and someone was in the middle of a eulogy. I found an empty seat in the rear. In a few moments it became very clear why it was so important for me to "happen" into this funeral.

The speaker, as it turns out, was the rabbi of the synagogue. Little did I know that he was about to say something I would never forget for the rest of my life:

> Mr. Schachner was a devout member of this syna-
> gogue. Every day he would dutifully attend services
> here — morning, afternoon, and night. He was a
> pious Jew, well liked by everyone who knew him.
>
> One morning, many years ago, when I left the
> synagogue, I walked outside and saw Mr.
> Schachner waiting across the street at a bus stop. I
> didn't think much of it. We exchanged greetings and
> I went on my way.
>
> The next morning the same scene repeated itself
> — as it did for several days consecutively. Until
> one day, I began to wonder, "Mr. Schachner lives
> around the corner. Why would he be waiting at the
> bus stop?" For some reason I was curious and I
> approached him with the question.
>
> "Since you live around the corner,' I said, "I won-
> der why you wait at a bus stop every day? Might
> you be going to work?"

I was totally unprepared for his answer.

> "No, Rabbi," he said. "I am retired and not going to
> work, and yes, I do live around the corner. But as
> you may know, I am a survivor of the Holocaust.
> For five dreadful years, I endured the most
> unspeakable horrors a human being can experi-
> ence. Most of the time, I was convinced that I
> would never see the true light of day again.
>
> "And then 1945 arrived — liberation. And life
> somehow had to begin anew. I had lost everything I
> had, but I made my way to America — penniless,

defeated, and alone. Slowly, I built a new life here — with strength that had long ago abandoned me.

"But I wondered about the Jewish People and their future. What would happen to them? How would they rebuild their glorious past and fulfill their destiny? It seemed nearly impossible. And yet, the answer was really not that complicated. I realized that it all boils down to one word. Education. We have to re-educate our People. Teach them the fundamentals of our belief and the beauty of our sacred Heritage. And we must start with the children. They are our future.

"I happened to be standing here, at this very bus stop, while I was pondering this thought...when a school bus rode by — filled with children on their way to school to study Torah.

"What a beautiful sight!' I thought. This is the future of our Nation. After a few more seconds another school bus drove by...and then another...and then another! And I started to count the busses. That day, Rabbi, I counted thirty-two school busses that I could see from that vantage point – all transporting Jewish children to study Torah. (Boro Park, after all.) What a spectacle!

"I was invigorated. So the next day, after services, I came out again, stood at this very same spot, and counted school busses. It became my ritual. Every morning I would start the day by counting school busses. And if one bus is missing for some reason, my day is ruined. That's why I stand here!"

Education.

The prerequisite to gaining access to the might that the seven keys have opened for you.

You see, without education you could have all the desire in the world; you could have full cognizance of how to be happy, what it means to have free will, the methodology of prayer and love, etc. — and still fall short of your potential. What you are missing is "information."

It's like buying a state of the art computer system, with the fastest processor created, the biggest hard drive in existence, and near-infinite memory. But if you leave the store without any software, all you have is a useless tower of chips. An eight-cylinder, 412 horsepower BMW is basically going nowhere without a tank of gas. That is the force that education carries.

Torah

It is the ultimate gift from God to the Jewish People. And appropriately, he called it Toras Chaim ... literally, *instructions for living.*

Today, everything you buy comes with an instruction manual, even a pen or a watch. And often, the manual is several inches thick, hundreds of pages long and written in a dozen different languages...because today we appreciate the complexity of even the smallest of inventions.

Life, you'll agree, is rather complex too. And God, in understanding that, decided that without a set of instructions for life, we'd be foundering and confused. And so, when the Jewish People were ready, in the year 2448 after Creation, in an unassuming location called Mount Sinai, God produced a National Revelation — witnessed by a constituency of three million plus people — and gave the Torah, both Written and Oral, to the Jews.

Its teachings are eternal; its messages profound. Its depth is astounding; its accuracy timeless; its splendor is unparalleled; its wisdom boundless.

The relevance of Torah — including every minute detail contain therein — makes the study of it the greatest commandment of all. The reason is obvious...because learning His words is knowing His will. It is the window through which He allows mortal mankind to peek and glimpse at the Ultimate. It is the wellspring of all the knowledge that ever was and ever will be accumulated in this limited and temporary world. There is no question that Torah does not answer. There is no question that Torah does not ask. It is all there — and it is up to us to find it.

Knowledge...information...wisdom...this is what allows us to understand our priorities and make appropriate decisions in everything we do.

Mitzvos

Torah is also God's chosen process of communicating His methodology to us so we can live our lives to our maximum potential.

The system He chose, in His infinite wisdom, is *mitzvos*, commandments.

This is hardly the forum to discuss the nature, purpose, and details of the 613 positive and negative commandments, along with the myriad Rabbinical instructions that further obligate us and enhance our connection to the Almighty. Scores of other books have dedicated themselves to exactly such a purpose.

Suffice it to say that the combination of mitzvah observance — much of which we may not entirely comprehend — and Torah study — which we strive to fully comprehend — comprises the nuts and bolts of the perfect formula for maximum pleasure in life.

"Where do I get some?"

The evolving process of how Torah and mitzvos have been transmitted through the ages has been nothing short of astounding. Let's review some of the chief stages of development right up to today:

- Step One, of course, was the aforementioned National Revelation at Mount Sinai that forged the basis of our belief in God forever.

- Step Two was the unique relationship between God and Moses, His hand-picked emissary. For forty years Moses learned directly, one on one, from God Himself. All the knowledge of Torah and mitzvos and, well, life itself, that would be needed for eternity was given over during that time.

- Step Three could be described as the oral transmission from Moses to Joshua and the Elders of Israel, of all the pertinent information needed for Torah study and mitzvah adherence.

- Just prior to the Jewish People entering the Land of Israel they received a complete written document of the Five Books of Moses, called the Written Law, which is an exact transcript of God's words to Moses. This text and the subsequent copies that were transcribed meticulously were used for study and reference by the populace. This would be Step Four.

- Step Five in our chain took place nearly 1,500 years later when Rabbi Judah the Prince boldly decided that due to centuries of persecution, war, disenfranchisement, and Temple destructions, the perils of forgetting our Oral teachings were so great that the Oral Torah needed to be committed to a written format. Thus was born the Mishnah and, 300 later later, Gemara — known together as the Talmud.

  Without a printing press, the primary mode of teaching and learning at that time was, of course, the oral process of teacher to student. Those communities that were fortunate enough to contain scholars of repute flourished in their level of scholarship and spiritual development.

- The invention of the printing process heralded in a new era of Torah proliferation — Step Six. Jews soon availed themselves of scores of monographs of varying degrees of Torah sophistication. They learned more, they wrote more, and they distributed their Torah. People in the furthest regions of the globe were soon able to develop their interests and erudition in ways never before possible.

- Step seven is the fairly recent phenomeon of English-language Judaica. Artscroll/Mesorah providing the world with excellent elucidations of the Talmud, Sccripture, liturgy and many other areas of our sacred heritage. Other publishers, such as Feldheim Judaica and Israel Book shop have published valued works in the vernacular. The result is an outstanding increase in worldwide Torah fascination and growth. While never intending to be an adequate substitute for the direct relationship between student and teacher, holy books on every aspect of Jewish life and spirituality, in many different languages, have become study tools for hundreds of thousands of Jews.

- In Step eight of our process, the use of taped recordings of Torah lectures and discourses meant that people could now learn while they traveled, washed dishes, or just sat at home, even though no teacher was available to offer instruction. Tens of thousands of Jews today also avail themselves of telephone services, such as TorahPhone and the Chofetz Chaim Heritage Foundation, as well as others, to listen to classes on every Jewish topic imaginable.

- Today thousands of *chavrusos*, study partners, learn on the phone at specified hours of the week, from all corners of the world. Partners in Torah is the organization that plays "matchmaker,"coordinating and setting up the study pairs.

- Many others attend seminars and weekend retreats (such as Aish HaTorah's Discovery,

Gateways, and Arachim), in which computer technology, and video techniques augment an incredibly dynamic learning process.

- Finally, Step nine is the Internet. While there is a plethora of offensive and even dangerous material on the net, and users must be very vigilant — especially where young people can access it — in the last few years, literally millions of Jews have utilized the World Wide Web as an instrument for Torah advancement. Everyone, from total beginners to scholars of high standing, can testify to the astonishing amount of wisdom available with the simple click of a mouse. The Aish HaTorah website alone — Aish.com — currently welcomes over 1.2 million "visits" each month! The Torah explosion is unprecedented!

In other words, there really are no more excuses not to learn Torah. No matter where you live, how often you travel, what your background, or what level of comprehension and familiarity you have reached, appropriate, relevant, and interesting topics are now readily available for your access.

The Jews are no longer in the desert.

▶ One final story

Let's conclude with one last story that should strike a chord in everyone.

It's the oft-told story about the fellow who has just taken a severe financial loss. After years of building a small fortune, he made an investment that turned sour and he lost it all. It does happen.

Desperate, he is driving along the highway and passes a racetrack.

"Who knows?" he thinks, "maybe this is my answer, my salvation."

He pulls over and goes inside.

Examining the program he notices one horse, Spatula, in the sixth race, that is listed at 3,000 to 1 odds. The gambit intrigues him.

*"If I use my last hundred dollars and Spatula some-
how wins the race, it will pay me $300,000!" he
reasons delusionally. "Stranger things have happened. I'll be back on my feet!"*

Impatiently he waits for the sixth race. His thoughts waft dreamily to his impending fortuity as he counts the ways he will spend his newfound fortune.

The time arrives. Spatula is still a 3,000 to 1 shot. Jubilantly, our hero strides to the window and wagers his last hundred dollars. He can nearly taste victory.

But a total fool, he is not. He realizes that a 3,000 to 1 shot probably could use a little help. And so he begins to pray.

*Oh, God, shine Your benevolence upon me and
upon Spatula. I need Your help so much. Just let
Spatula get out of the gate together with the other
nine horses. Maybe if she gets off to a good start, it
will give her confidence.*

And so it happens. The gate flies open and the frenzied contestants charge onto the track. Spatula is with them.

*"Oh, thank you, Almighty for giving me hope," he
continues. "Now, if only You could keep her at pace
with the others...so she doesn't lose desire — even
for 30 seconds or so."*

Once again, the prayer is answered, as Spatula valiantly gallops to the middle of the pack. Our hero's eyes are starting to widen. The fantasy is still alive. And so, his prayers intensify. He can hardly get the words out.

*I am so grateful for everything You've done for me,
O Lord. Leading me to this incredible opportunity,
creating the scenario, and now keeping Spatula in
the mix. The race is half over, as You know, and
perhaps it is time for this Philly to make her move.
Could I impose upon You to push her to the front*

*— even just by a nose? Let her get a taste of being
in the lead!*

Sure enough, within seconds, Spatula surges to the front. The crowd is in shock. They rise to their feet. A 3000 to 1 shot is leading the race! Once again, our friend turns heavenward. This thing could really happen!

*My appreciation knows no bounds, God. Who
would have imagined such a thing possible? Of
course, leading by a nose means nothing. If only
she could pull away from the others — just a bit,
say, a length or two. Now that would really be
something! It's in Your hands, God. Please! Please
show me Your power!*

Incredibly, Spatula quickens her pace. The other horses seem no match for this daring animal as her lead reaches two full lengths! With only one short stretch left to the race, one final, desperate prayer is offered.

*"I have no words left," he mumbles nearly incoherently. "I'll never forget You for this. But the race is
not over. Others horses are still within reach!"*

He is sweating profusely now. His plea is frantic. His voice is cracking.

*Putting Spatula five lengths ahead right now would
seal the victory! Do it! Please do it!*

To his utter amazement, Spatula forges ahead by five lengths. Only seconds separate him from the finish line.

Our hero drops into his seat, surveys the scene around him, looks up and says calmly:

Okay, God, I can take it from here.

Frankly, the story is a silly one. Betting the ponies will never get you anywhere, except in deeper trouble. But the lesson from this old yarn is poignant and priceless.

How many of us really do the same thing? When we need help, we turn to God. When things look desperate, we turn to God. When there's nowhere else to turn, we turn to God. But when things are fine, when times are going well, when good fortune surrounds us, we turn to ourselves. We are proud. We pat ourselves on the back and say, "Nice going!" Credit? Always. Blame? Never.

How sad. God is not Superman. He doesn't appear out of nowhere to catch you from a falling building and then disappear before all the reporters show up. He doesn't answer 911 when an emergency occurs and then retreat to the ambulance garage. God is ALWAYS with us. Guiding...teaching...navigating...opening our eyes so that we see His power, feel His love, and bask in His Presence.

Reminder

We have made a strong pitch for the study of Torah and for mitzvah observance. But beware. Beware of the "all or nothing" syndrome.

So many people, enlightened by the prospect of infusing some spirituality into their lives, leap into these new vistas of education and performance, only to find themselves "burned out" quickly. Primarily it is because the demands are so vast, the material so infinite, and the mountain so tall that they cannot envision reaching the summit. And so, unable to "get it all," they end up with nothing.

What a pity. That is not the Jewish way.

Every step you take is precious. Every word you study is a building block. Every single m itzvah is a precious gem...to be refined and treasured. No one "gets it all." The climb to the heavens takes forever...and then some.

Just remember that you've been down this road before. The first time, you were accompanied by an angel. He took you to the top and then gently asked you to start the trip over again.

Now you walk with God.

Enjoy the journey.